Drawing and Painting

FACES AND FIGURES

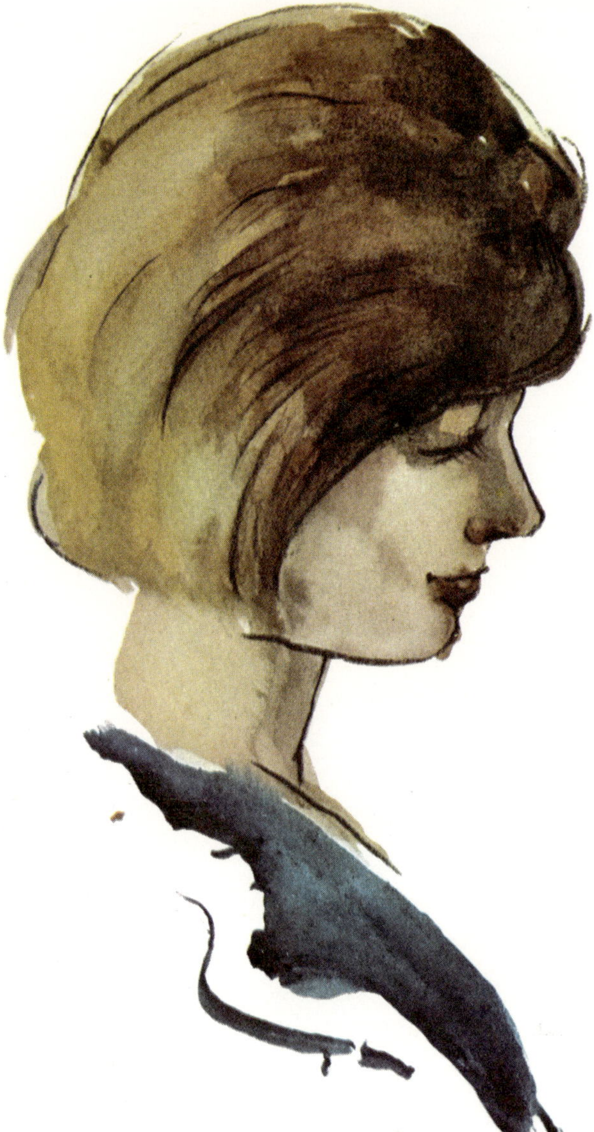

Profile in carbon and watercolour.

Drawing and Painting

FACES AND FIGURES

written and illustrated by

ADRIAN HILL

P.R.O.I., R.B.A.

LONDON

BLANDFORD PRESS

First published in 1962
Second impression 1971

167 High Holborn, London, WC1V 6PH

ISBN 07137 0026 2

For

RUTH AND DUDLEY SOMMER

Printed in Great Britain by
Fletcher & Son Ltd, Norwich
Colour illustrations printed by
Jarrold & Sons Ltd, Norwich

Contents

ILLUSTRATIONS IN COLOUR

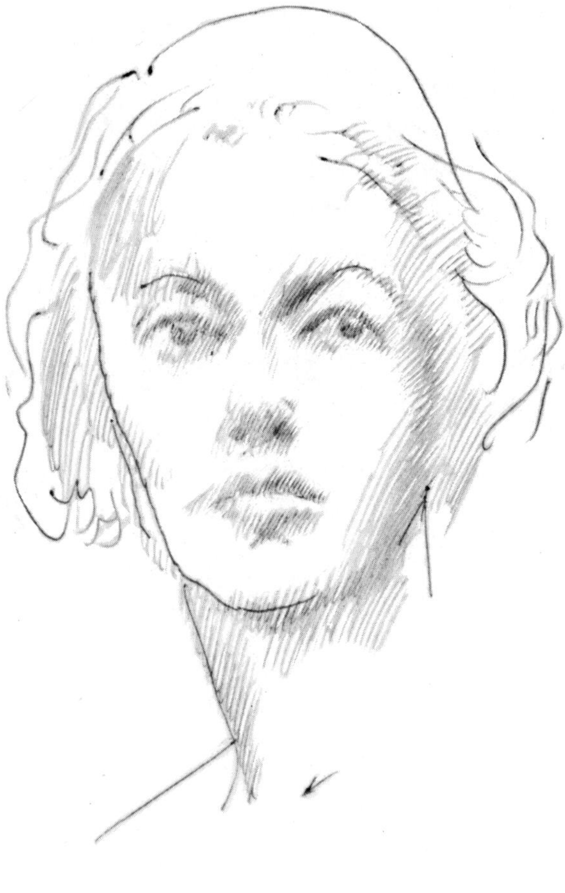

Direct ball point pen drawing.

ILLUSTRATIONS IN BLACK AND WHITE

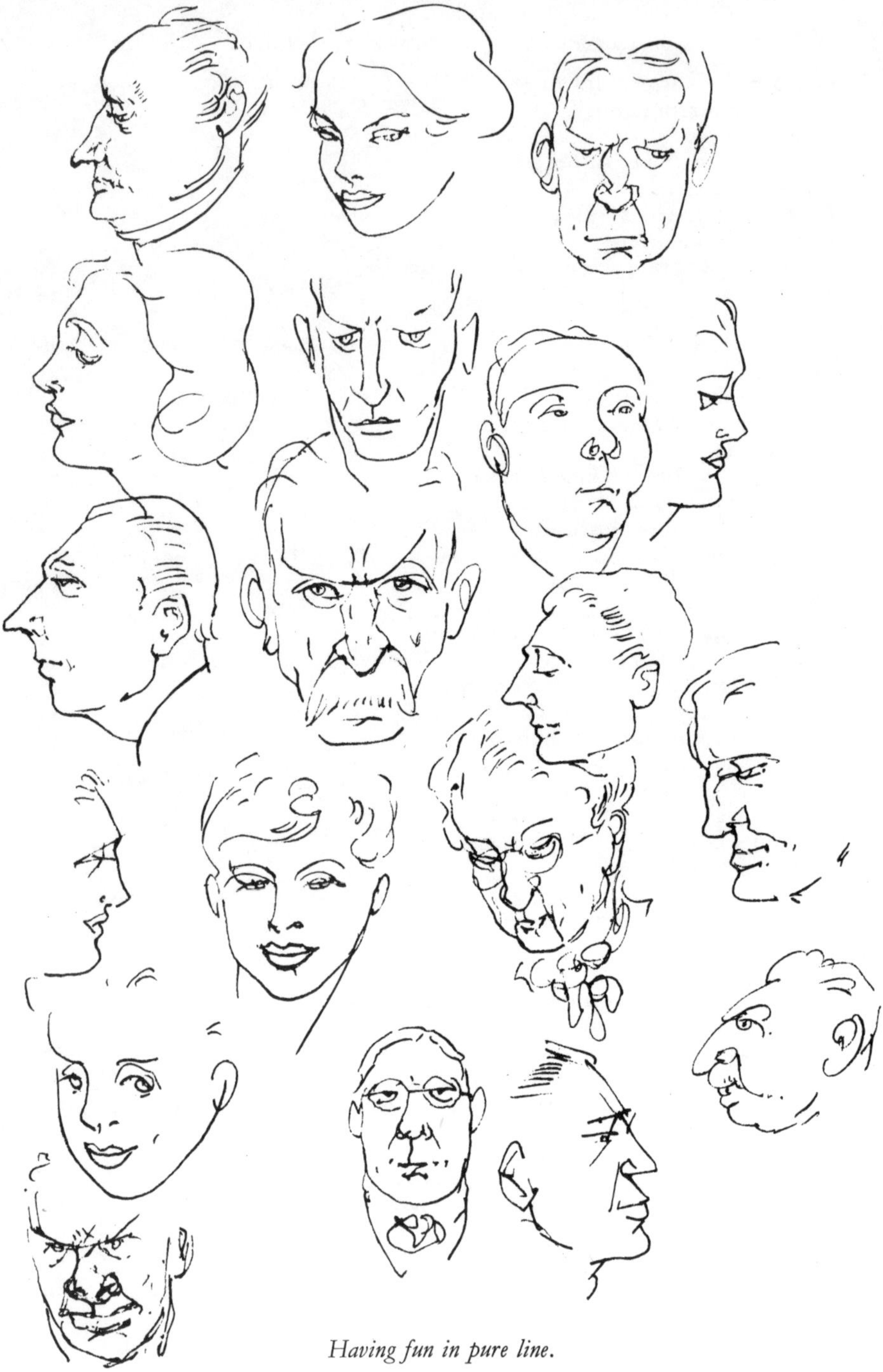

Having fun in pure line.

Introduction: Faces

PORTRAITURE at the present time has been declared "a languishing Art", and a recent pronouncement called it "a lost Art". Yet after many years' teaching experience, especially in the field of amateur or non-vocational Art, it would appear that portrait painting, or if that implies too professional a standard, painting heads, remains one of the most popular lines to pursue, despite the fact that it remains one of the most exacting to perform successfully.

(In the best sense of that very overworked word, drawing and painting faces, is still envisaged as *great fun.*)

Whether this desire derives from a love of humanity or stems from a disinclination to paint out of doors—which is implicit in the practice of landscape—is a moot point. Be that as it may, I have often heard the veriest tyro express an ambition to be able to paint faces, and this, in the face—the simile is appropriate—of a formidable number of technical problems, which have to be surmounted before there is any chance of this hope being gratified.

A face to be like one, demands more than the "slap-happy" approach which the child adopts (although many of these results have their quota of naivety and consequent charm). This lack of technique has nothing to recommend it when we no longer see and record visual facts through the "innocent eyes" of unsophisticated youth.

No, the promised "fun" must be preceded by that other sort of fun which stems from the spade-work of study. Indeed such study as faces require will be found to be all absorbing and all rewarding, not only I would say in the purely pictorial results, but in our revaluation of human feelings, emotions and behaviour. Certainly nothing teaches us more about how to use our eyes than when we essay to portray the expressive eyes of others, for it is surely through these lamps of character that lurks the true personality of the sitter, and a true portrait of that particular person is rendered.

And in this specialized Art—as it will certainly be found to be—I would stress that drawing *must* precede painting.

Without a sound constructional foundation of drawing, your painting of the head will lack all proportion and character and indeed all the essentials that make it a living breathing human face.

To achieve this proficiency, we must start at the beginning and we must start with the shape.

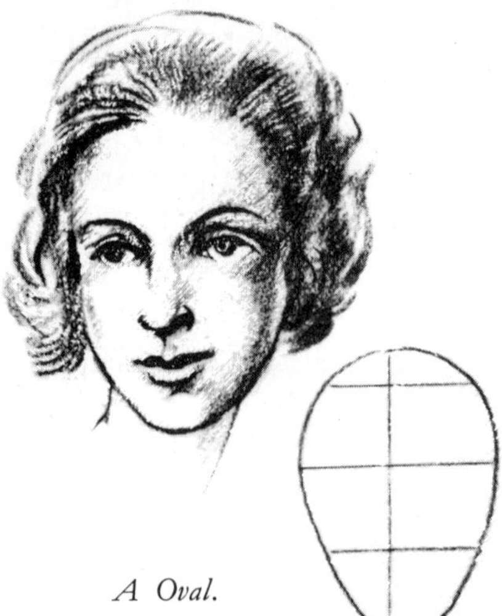

A Oval.

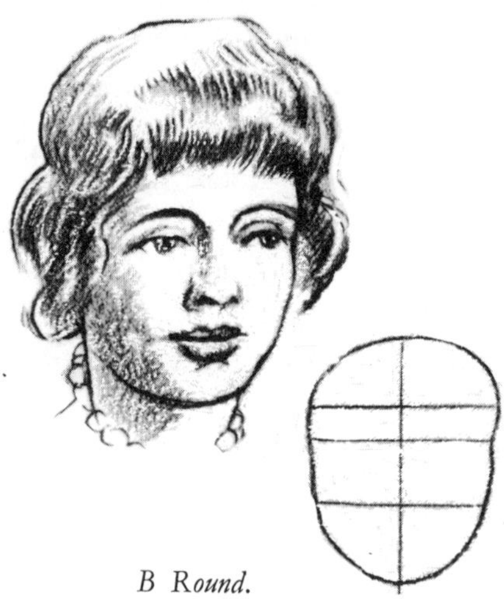

B Round.

In the female head hair fashion often determines the length and breadth of forehead.

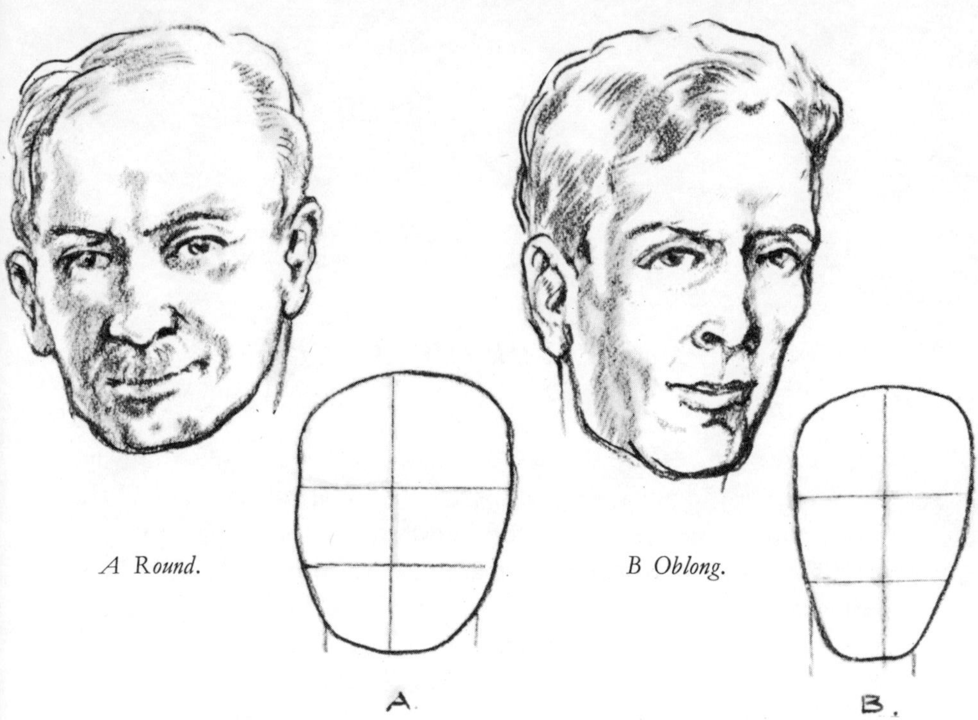

Note the relative length of forehead, nose and chin to the breadth of face.

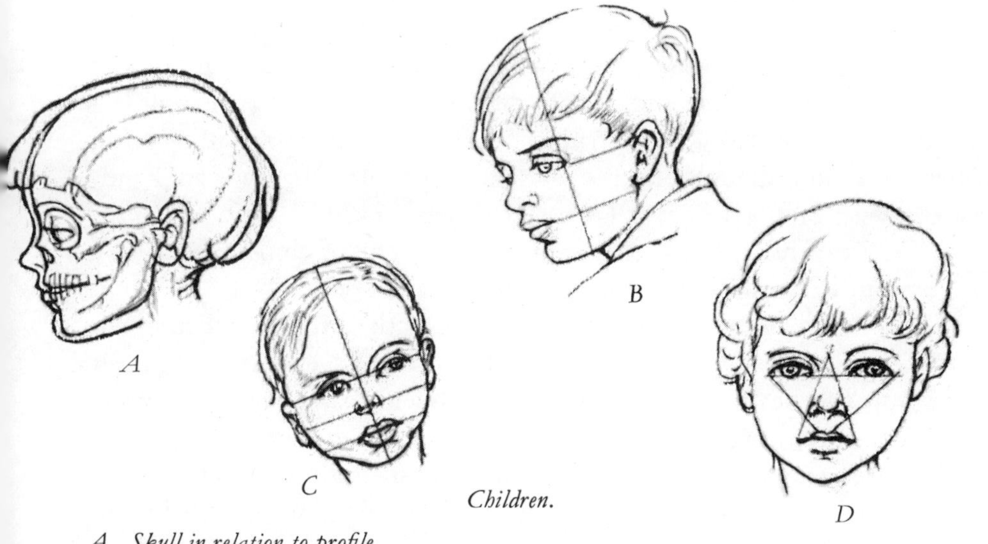

Children.

A *Skull in relation to profile.*

B *Relative distances from corner of eye and mouth to ear, and eye to top of head and base of chin.*

C *Length of facial area to cranium.*

D *Lines to check length and breadth of features.*

I Drawing Faces

NO two faces are the same shape. That is the first thing to realize and always remember. Even identical twins, on close inspection, have some very subtle differences of shape and very slight variations in form and feature. Nature never repeats herself exactly. In more ordinary people these personal characteristics are self-evident, their faces can be said to be square or oval, round or long, their noses are long or short, their eyes small and deep-set or large and wide apart, their chins strong or weak. They are high or low browed, with all that that implies! We generally describe people in round terms by saying they are dark or fair, tall or short; that is easy, but when we really attempt to describe the face and go into details, we realize how difficult it is sometimes to give a true picture by word of mouth—words meaning different things to different people. But if we are handy with our pencil, it is far easier to pass on information—i.e. the sort of nose, the kind of mouth, the shape of chin—especially if our drawing is a profile view. Try it and see!

Incidentally I defy anyone to state with authority whether the set of one's own wife's, husband's, or child's, ears is high or low in the head. Ears can display as much character as any other feature, but these unfortunate organs, being taken for granted, are generally neglected in drawing heads, and so often of poor quality when closely looked at in a finished painting. It is important therefore to remember that *every* feature has its own shape

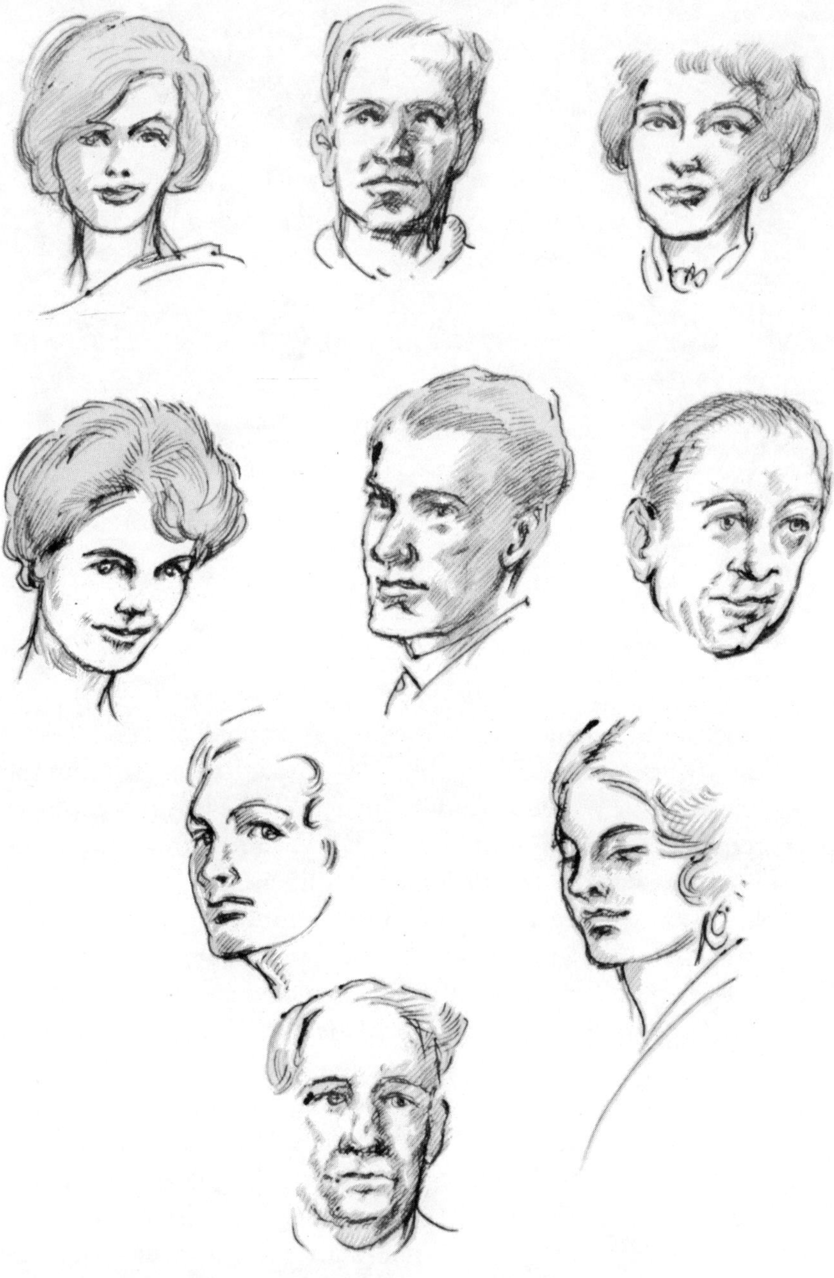

Loosening up with direct pen drawings in line and shade.

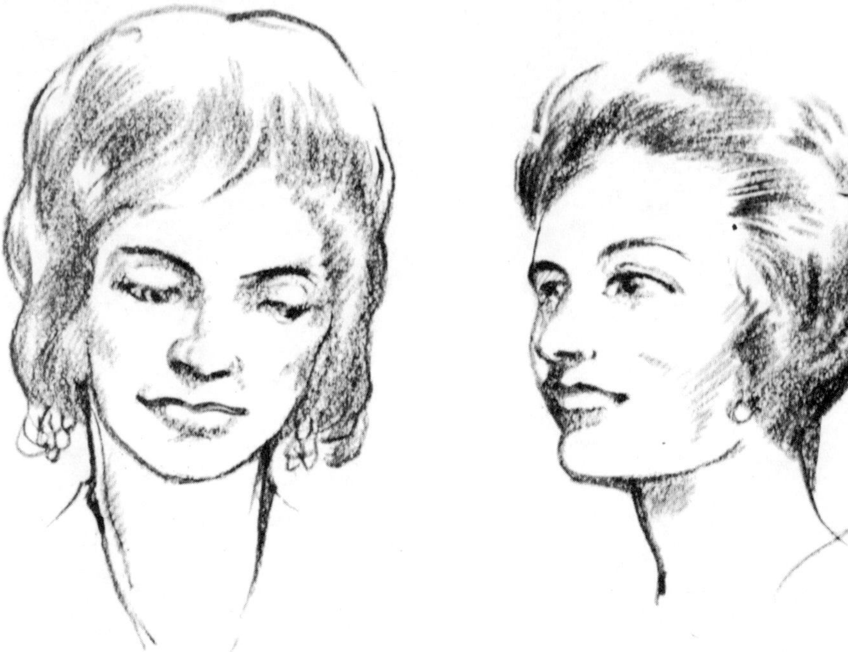

The downward look is often characteristic of the type of sitter—as is the lift in the eyes of another.

and each in its way and turn adds up to a true likeness.

And if ever a cliché fits the bill, it is the axiom of "painting the particular while remembering the general", for it is this problem of remembering the solid shape while concentrating on the features that wins in the struggle for a likeness.

Now I know there are definite, fool-proof symbols for drawing features—the eyes are suggested in a certain way, the nose indicated by certain "touches", the lips depicted by a slick gesture. They are no more than traditional devices which with a little practice anybody can copy. Armed with these pictorial signs, drawing faces is a pleasant enough but mechanical process, which is proved quite inadequate just as soon as you wish to draw, not just anybody's face, but a particular one and make it a likeness! It is then that these conventional symbols fail to correspond to a *particular feature*. The sign for the nose does not represent the nose of your sitter, the foolproof prototype for the eyes fails to represent the particular "look" of those eyes which confront you and the whole artifice falls apart. And it is time it did, for otherwise there would be no attempt at "getting a likeness".

For there is no doubt that the closer we follow the exact nature and growth of the individual feature, and the more we strive to draw it in our way, the better chance we have of making the face *like* the one we are drawing.

How often when our version of the sitter and the original are compared the speculation arises—there is something wrong about the slant of the nose, the curve of a nostril, the set of the eyes. What is it? Such problems which will always arise, are discussed and explained better by illustration in this and the following chapters.

On the other hand it is fatally easy in striving for a likeness to forget to construct a good *solid* head, which can be seen to *go round*. And that must be our first aim—not only must the shape be correct, but it must be a solid shape.

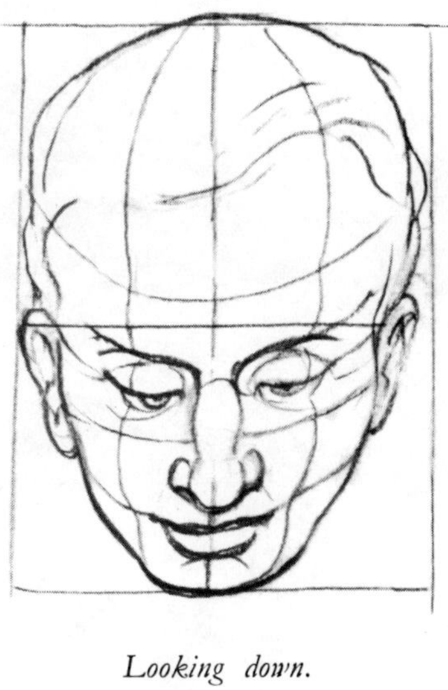

Looking down.

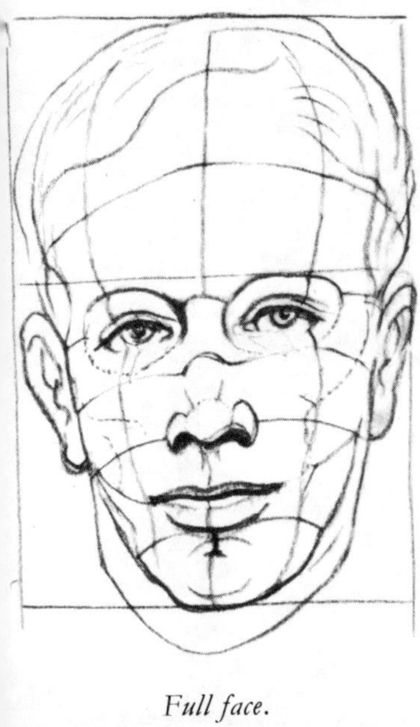

Full face.

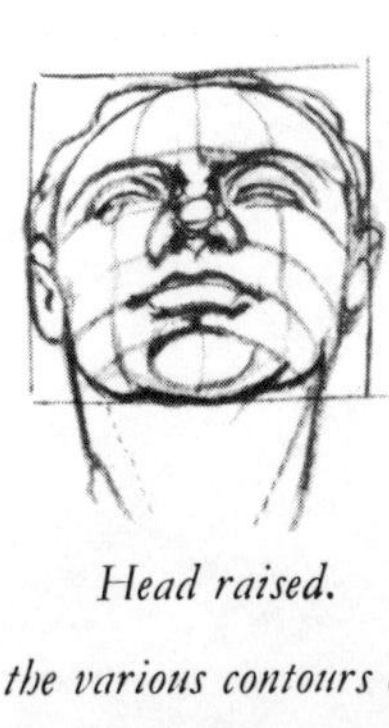

Head raised.

Showing the various contours of the face.

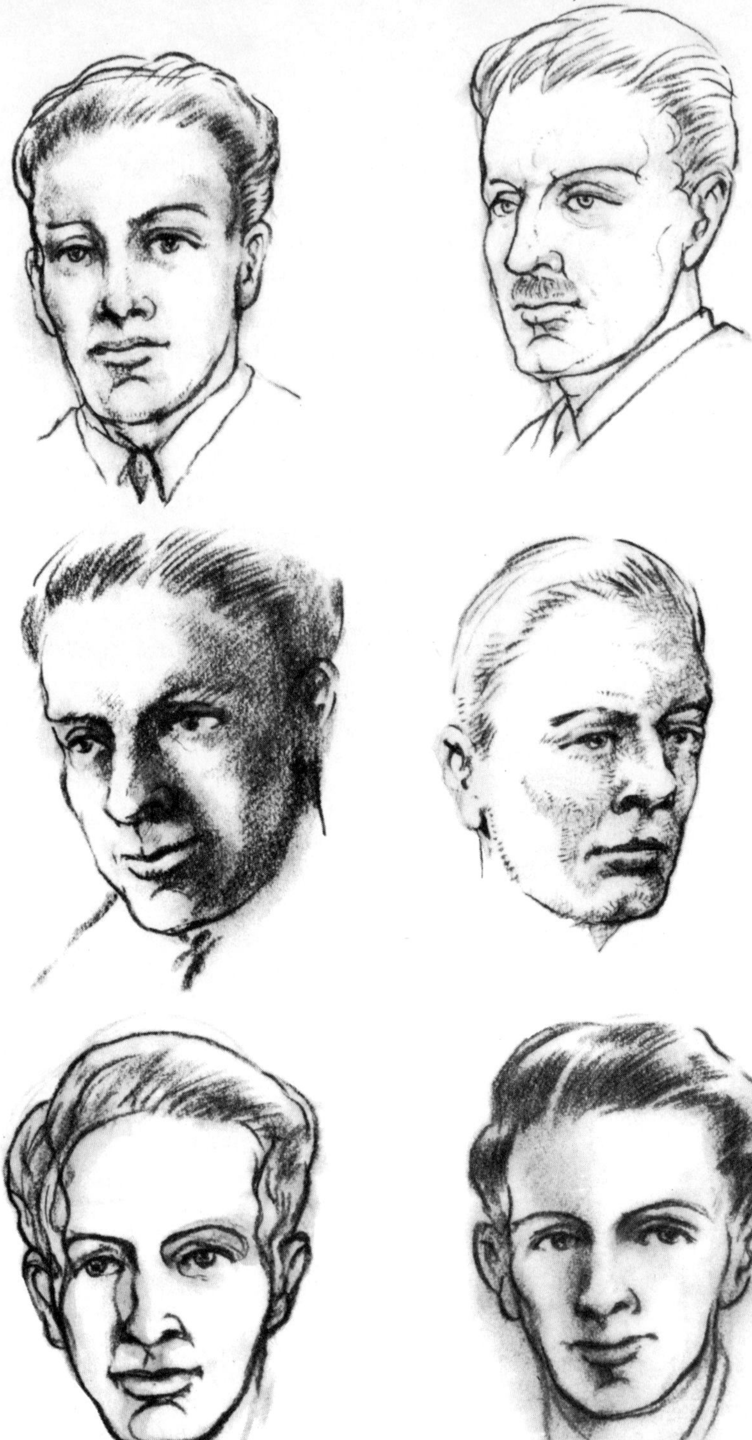

Various techniques in portraying male types.

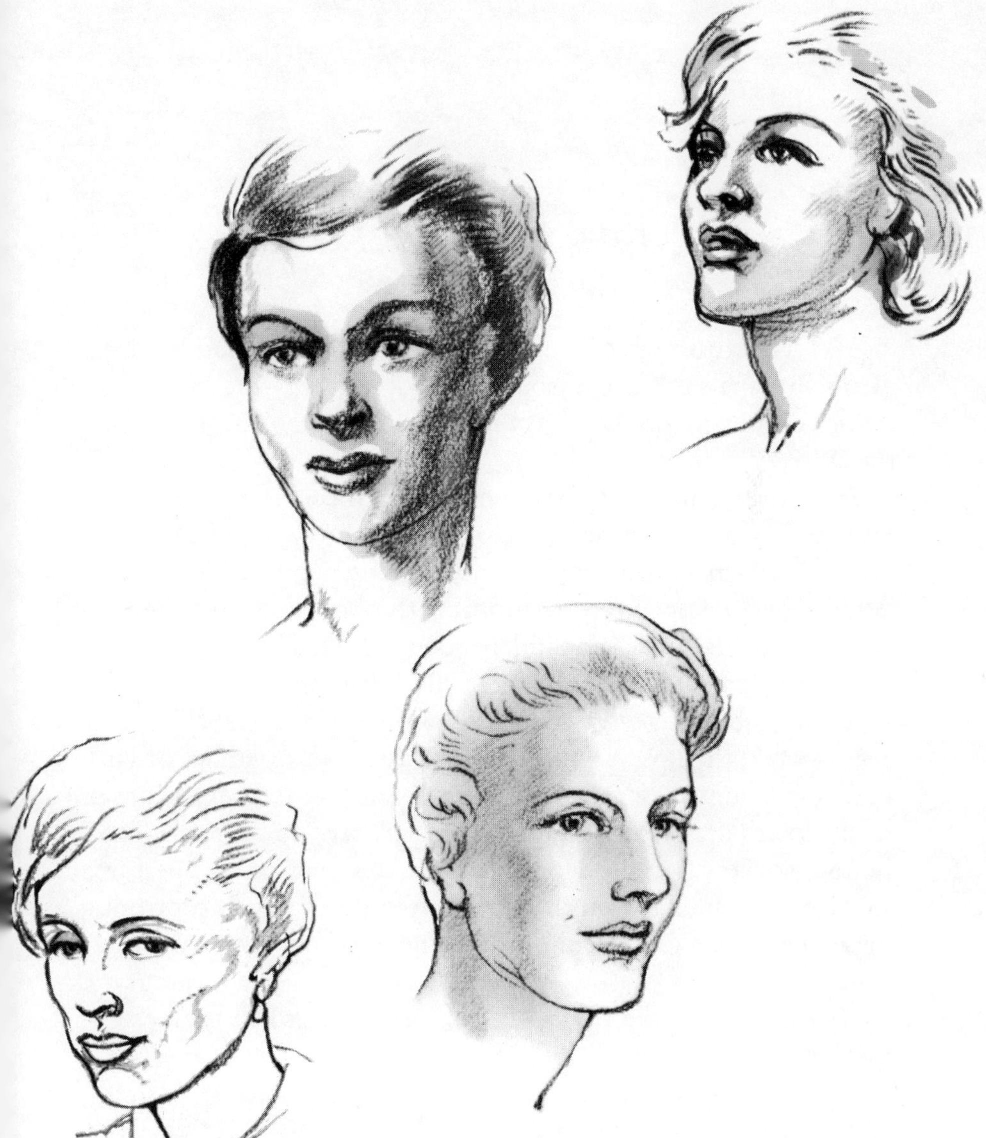

Various techniques in portraying female types.

2 *The Face in Detail*

EACH feature which goes to make up a solid rounded face will repay a close inspection, not only in the way it is fashioned but in the way in which it functions. The How and the Why.

Take the comparative movements of the eyes and lips for example. When we close the former, it is the *upper* lid or fleshy "blind" which comes down to cover the pupil, while in the latter, when we open our mouth, it is the *lower* lip which *descends*. And this operation is not independent like the eye movement, but is performed by the *lowering* of the *bottom jaw*.

While only the *pupils* of the eye move in their sockets and *move together*, the lips varying in shape can pout or smile, or curl or droop in unison or independently, as when we twist up a corner of the lower lip. Again, while the eyes are seen to be *inserted* into hollow sockets and the mouth can cause a vent or an aperture, the nose is a *projection* on the surface, the tip of which protrudes beyond the brow and chin, while the ears are "*hung on*" each side.

Finally we only see the *full* "*face*" of the ear when the head is turned *sideways*.

In short, the eyes are *embedded*, the nose is a *wedge*, the mouth is a *slit* and the ears are *appendages*! Now each feature pays for being studied separately, for each is differently *constructed*, varying according to sex, character and age (see illustrations).

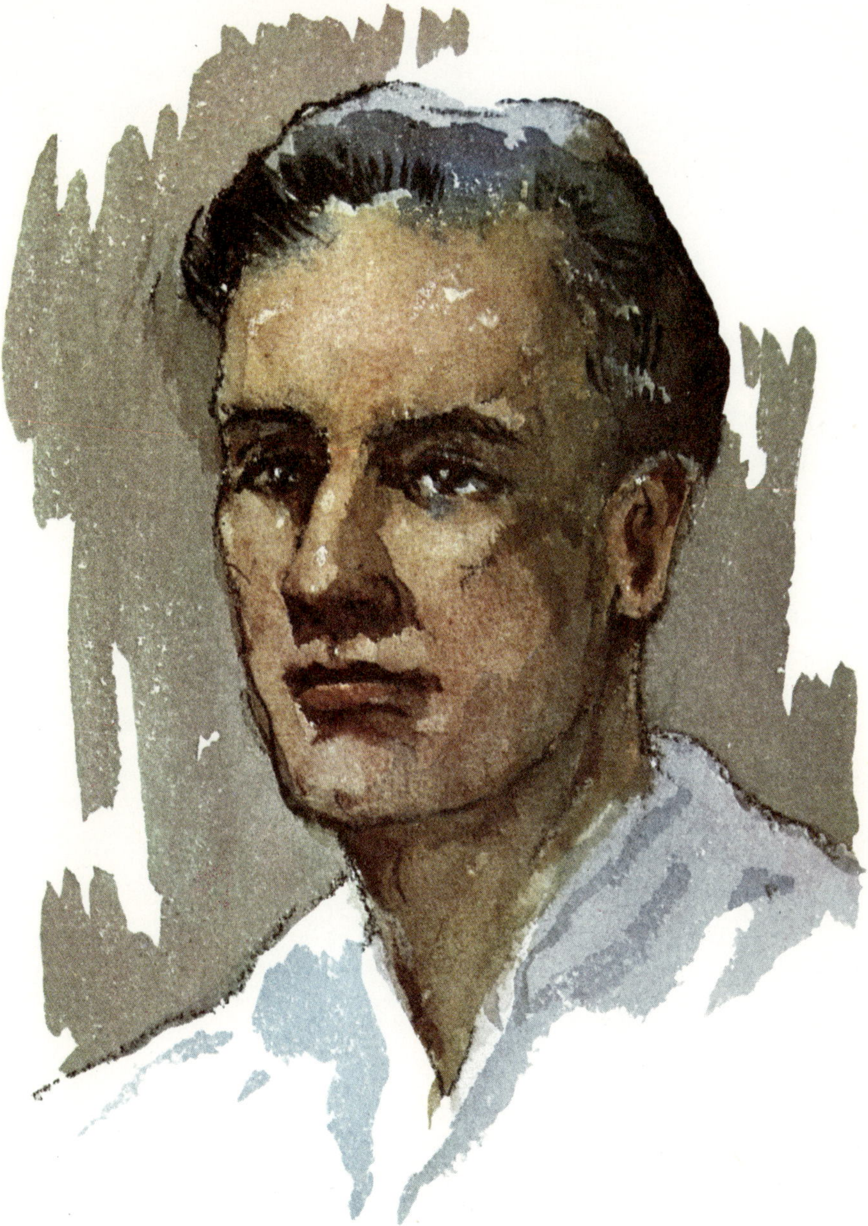

Features painted in while the previous wash is still damp. Outline strengthened.

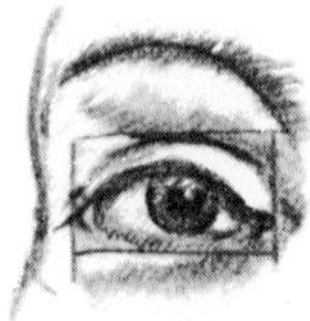

Three-quarter.

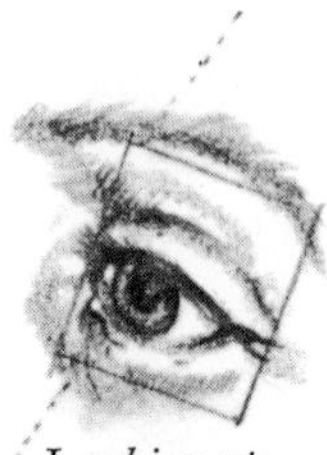

Looking up.

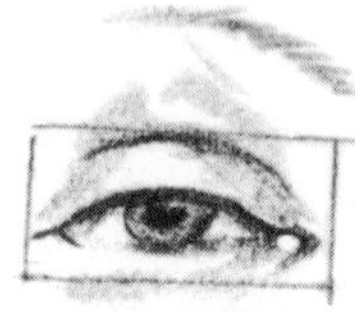

Half closed.

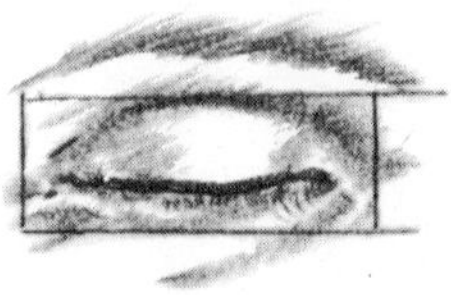

Closed.

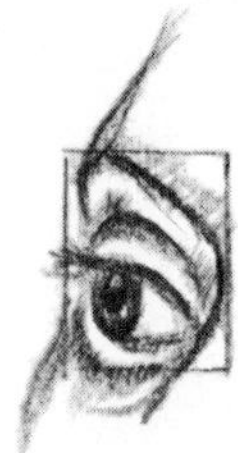

Near profile.

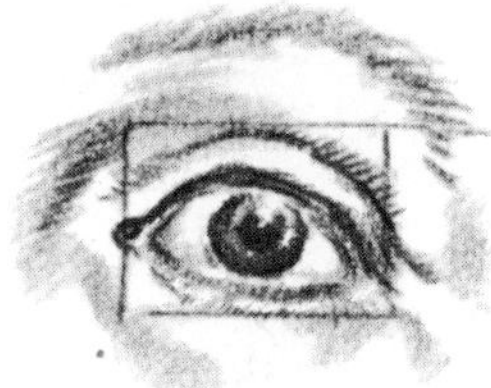

Wide open.

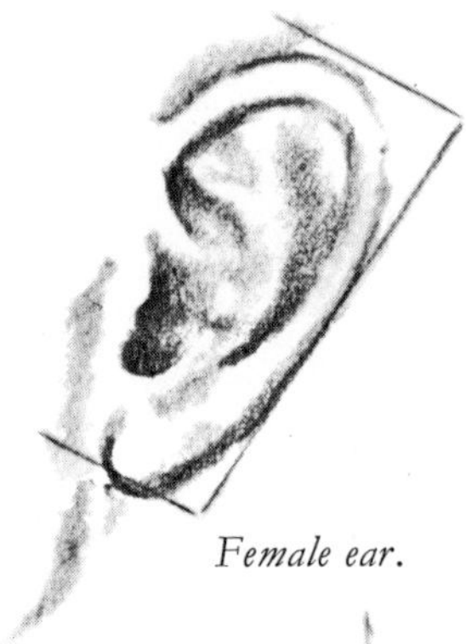

Female ear.

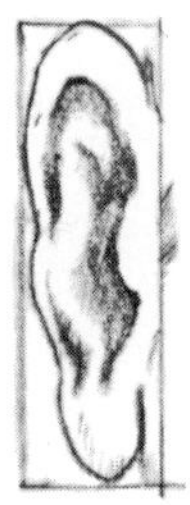

Front view.

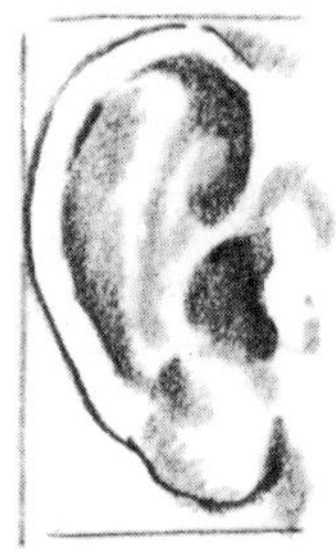

Male ear.

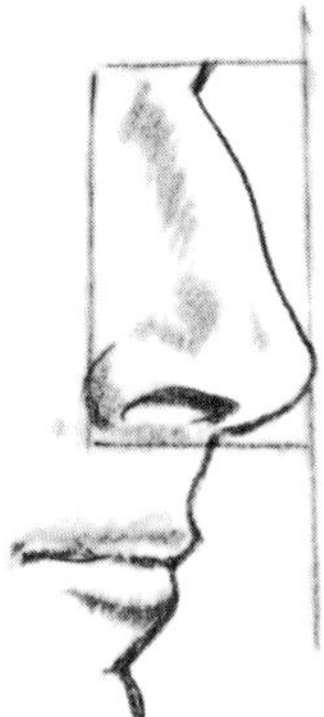

Side view.

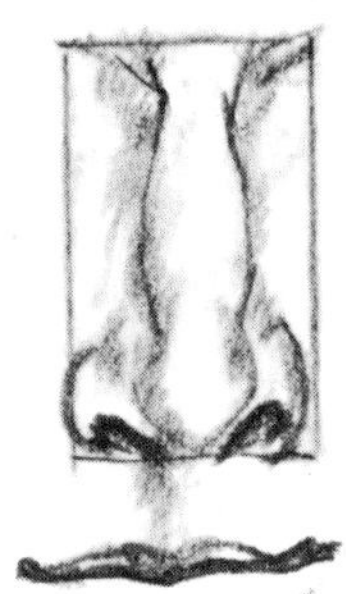

Front.

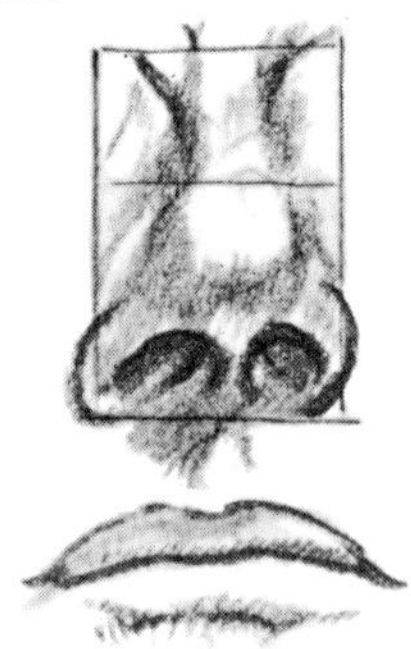

Raised.

Eyes and Ears and Nose.

The nose of the infant remains but a "smudge" when the ears are fully formed, while in extreme old age, the nose is the last feature to be changed by time—indeed in many cases it becomes more developed as the remaining bones of the head shrink.

Does not all this detail inquiry rob the actual drawing of its freshness? I do not think so, for the more we know about what we are drawing, the more in character our drawing will resemble that of our sitter. By our distinctive features are we known to be individuals, and knowledge of this will surely promote confidence and ultimate freedom of expression.

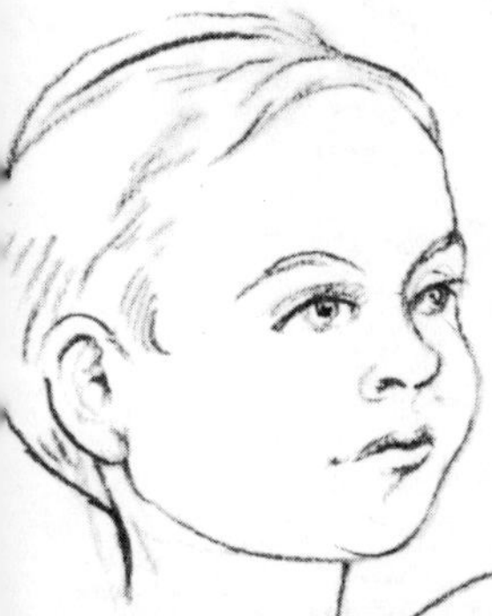

Youth.

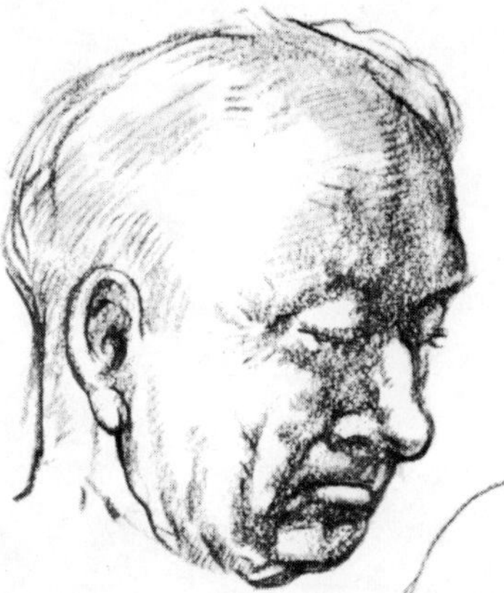

Age.

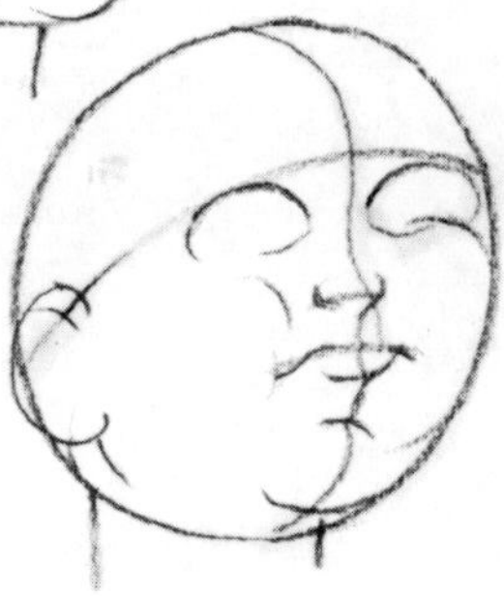

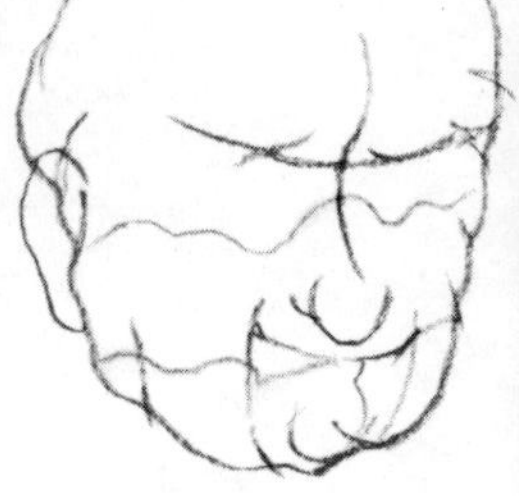

This becomes this.

I hope that the accompanying illustrations will present such studies as an enjoyable undertaking rather than a boring task. It is after all the answer to the questions, "Why is A unlike B?" And "Why does C remind us of D?" And the artist has it in his power (when he knows his job) to answer these questions not only correctly but with artistic integrity, i.e. *his way*.

Caricature can play a useful part in portraying character. For our purpose however it is a matter of emphasis rather than comic exaggeration or distortion. The crude caricature merely pokes fun and makes for the ridiculous. Pure caricature as such is always unkind and often downright cruel! We may laugh (and generally do) at the caricatures of others, even perhaps of our friends, but behind the cover of a wry smile we resent it when we ourselves

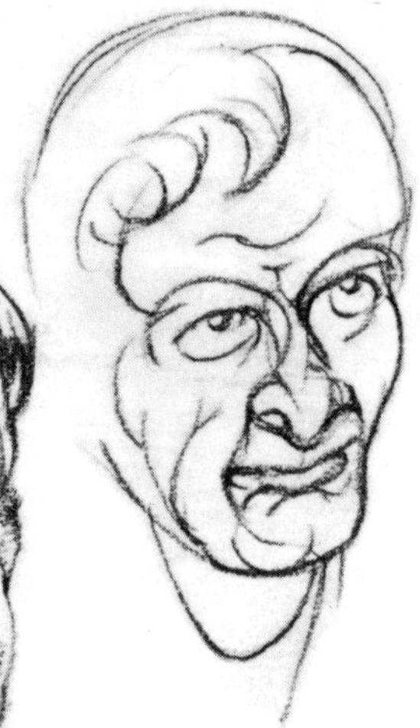

B *Stressing the type, personal treatment.*

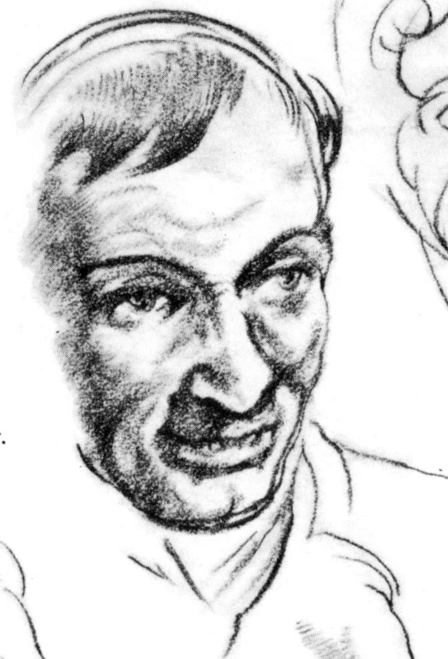

A *Stating the facts.*

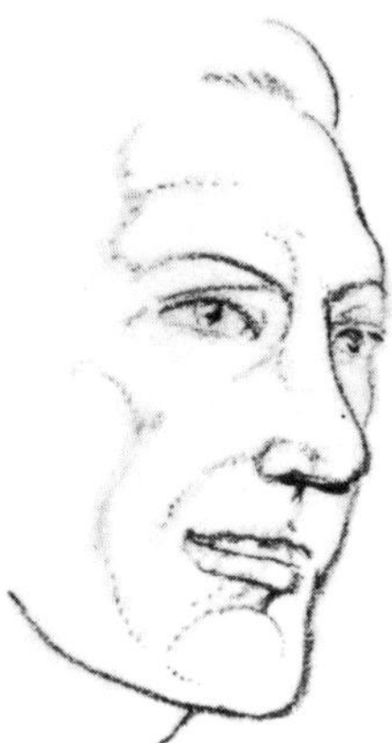

C *Portrayal of character by dotted line and accent.*

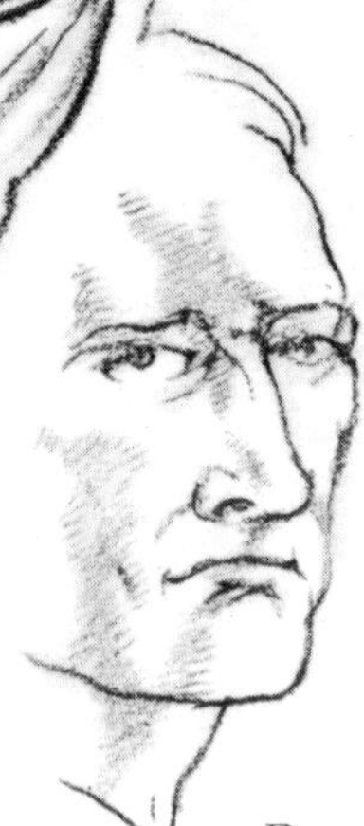

D *Portrayal of character by diagonal line shading.*

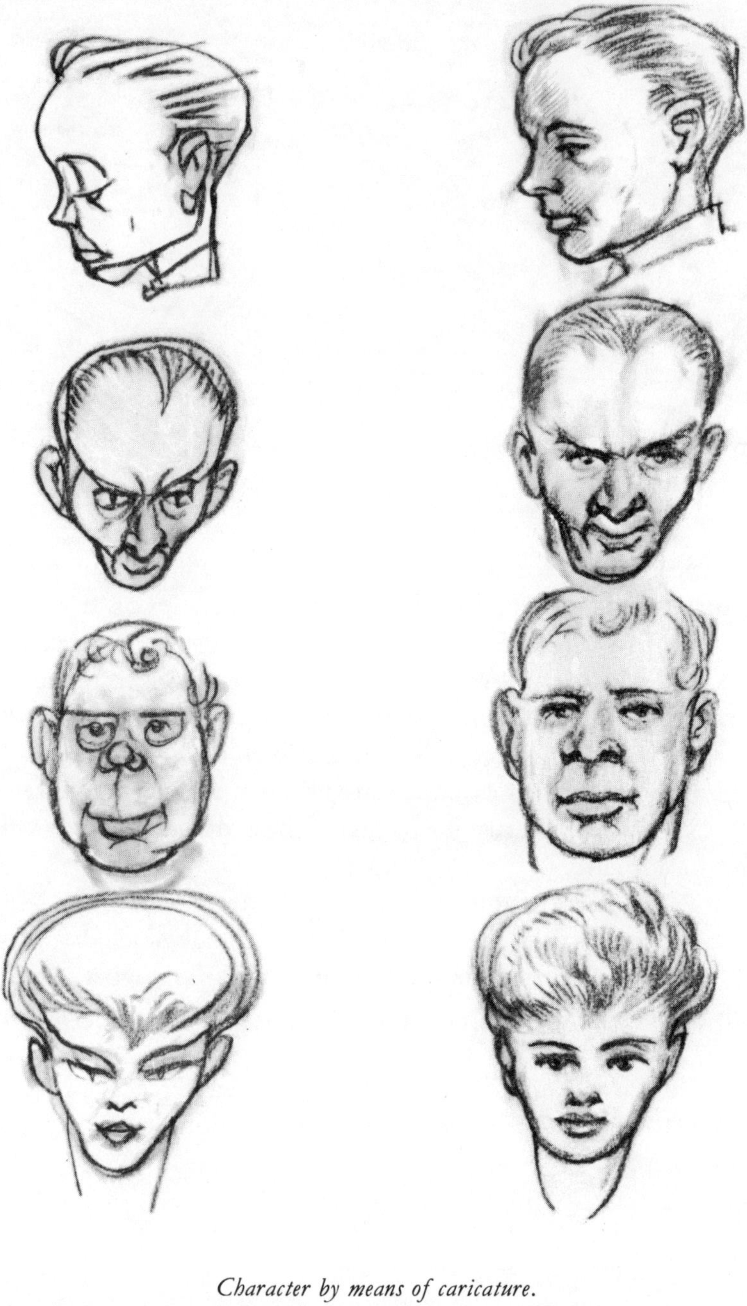

Character by means of caricature.

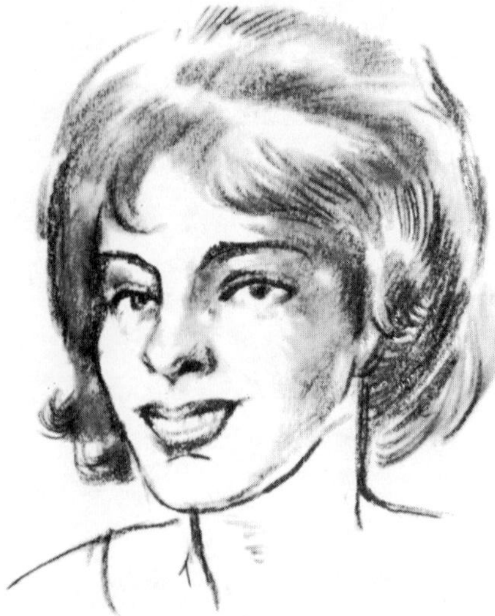 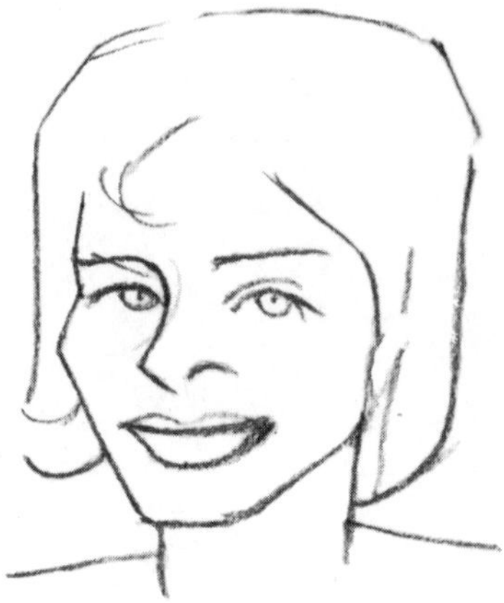

are caricatured. This is very natural. Once the portrait painter has diagnosed as it were the, let us say, peculiarities or "irregularities" in his sitter's face, a very subtle suggestion by accent or even colour can without a trace of mockery bring out the true character, whether it be a loveable trait or a hint of reserve, pride or even disdain. The examples I have given will, I hope, demonstrate how, by means of caricature, we can assess the degree of pictorial emphasis necessary to reveal these distinctive characteristics in our sitters.

Comic faces and funny figures, on the other hand, by which the cartoonist arrives at his "joke" are generally such a travesty of human nature that they can hardly be said to be worth serious study. But even in this playful field the political cartoonists like Low, Giles and Furber by sheer wit and satire often manage to reconcile the true and the ridiculous and hence reach an artistic result. Mostly, however, it is sufficiently venomous to remain a lampoon.

3 *The Technical Approach (Oil Painting)*

CHARCOAL is the best medium for the preliminary drawing of a painting to be done in oils. The line is precise and smooth and can be repeatedly corrected by wiping off with a soft rag, and as with the beginner corrections are inevitable and numerous, a suitable and effective method of erasure is very important.

Anything approaching detailed drawing of the features in this first stage is to be avoided, but proportion is absolutely essential if your head is in any way to resemble your sitter!

The correct placing of the head on your canvas or board should be the first concern. In a full face the intersection of diagonal lines drawn from the four corners should help to determine the position between the nose and the chin. Without this simple device, the head can so easily be drawn in too low and will consequently lose dignity.

If a side view is preferred, slightly more background should be allowed *in front* of the head than that which is seen behind.

The same unequal spacing should be observed if a three-quarter pose has been chosen.

In both cases the head should appear a little off-centre.

The constructional lines should now determine the correct proportions, i.e. length and breadth of forehead to length from the eye brows to the tip of the nose, and depth from the wing of the nostril to the angle of the jaw.

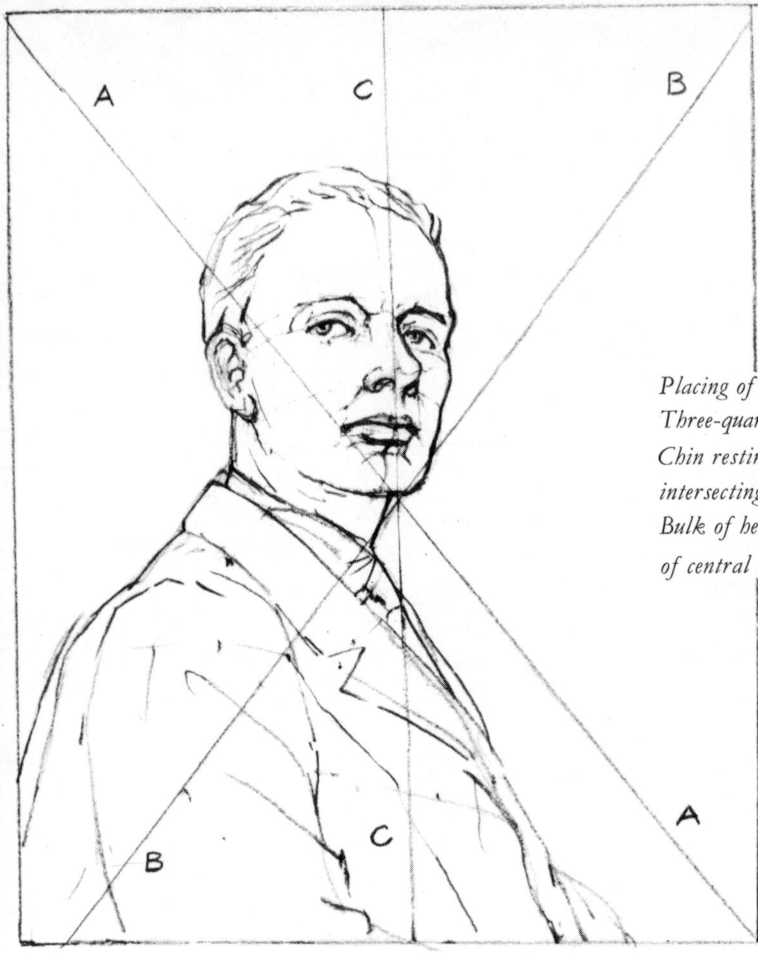

Placing of the head. Three-quarter view. Chin resting on the intersecting diagonals A, B. Bulk of head to the left of central line C.

In a three-quarter view, particular care must be taken with the slant of the nose, outline of forehead, cheek bone and chin and in the foreshortening of the lips.

It is fatally easy without these checks to make the nose too long and the eyes too close together or too wide set, or even on different levels!

It is only when these various points have been checked (and rechecked if necessary) that your charcoal lines can be safely fixed (with charcoal fixative) and you can embark on the actual painting, for when this is in progress, the individual features can often get enlarged unless their boundaries are firmly and

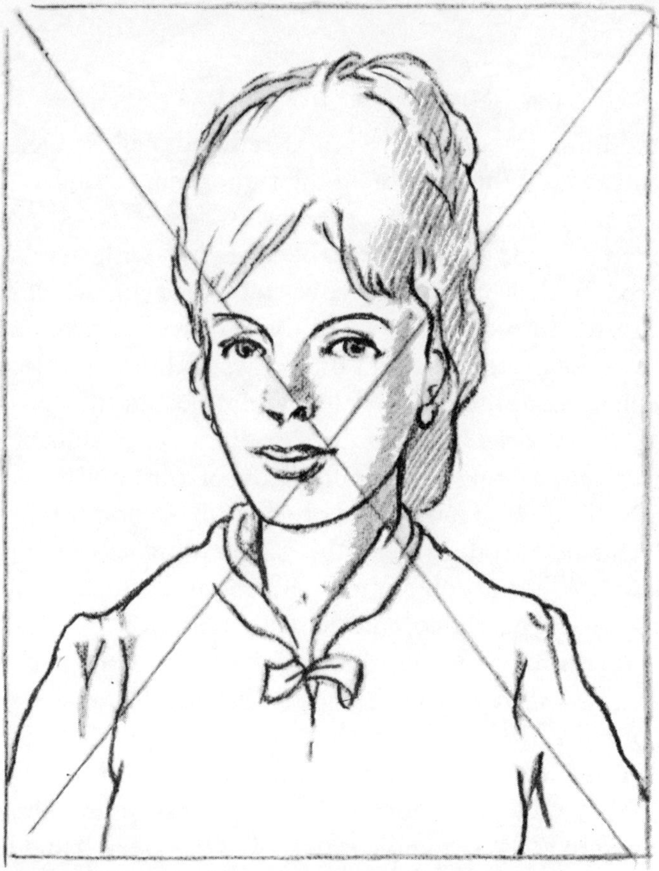

Here the chin is lower than the half-way line because of the hair style, the top of which must not touch the top of the canvas.

accurately established. As to the stages which follow, there is a variety of courses open, for no two painters adopt the same procedure. While some students only enjoy complete freedom if no conditions are imposed and no "holds barred" in getting (or trying to get) results, there are others who only gain confidence if guided to their goal.

One suggested line of action is to mix with plenty of turps an all over flesh tint which corresponds to the sitter's complexion and rub this all over the area of the face, transparent enough to see the charcoal markings of the features underneath.

This tint, according to whether the sitter be dark or fair, can be made up by mixing a little light red and Yellow Ochre with sufficient Flake White to obtain the right tone, adding a touch of black to soften or "degrade" the tint.

Next the shadow forms can be *rubbed in* with a mixture of light red and Terra Vert—covering the eyes, which can be painted back into this tone when the features are taken up later. They will then retreat behind the brows and ridge of nose.

The hair (an approximate colour only) should then be (again I use the word) *rubbed* in, for all these tints will result in what is called under-painting, as a foundation of tint and tone for the final modelling with more solid brushwork. In no portion should high lights be introduced, but the darker passages of the hair can be stated boldly and sometimes will be found sufficient in texture to suffice for a nearly completed statement.

It is then time to match the tint and tone of the background which can be allowed to overrun the outline of the face for then you can paint the outside flesh tones *back* into the background and effect a blending of the two and thus overcome the problem of edginess. When the shoulders (line of dress or coat) have been thinly painted in your whole canvas will be covered and you can see the whole portrait in terms of general colour and tone. It is dangerous to attempt a definite ruling as to the following stages —whether you "take up" the eyes first or work downwards from the forehead to the chin, or "flit" from feature to feature— for nobody, as I said, works exactly alike, but it is safe to give a warning: your painted head will "close up" all too quickly, and in order to prevent it from becoming tight—keep your brush strokes broad and eschew detail to the very last. The high lights on forehead, tip of nose, in the pupils of the eyes and that deft liquid touch on the lips—they can only be effective when applied with a small brush as *finishing* touches. Be careful not to over-do wrinkles in the forehead, or round the eyes, especially the

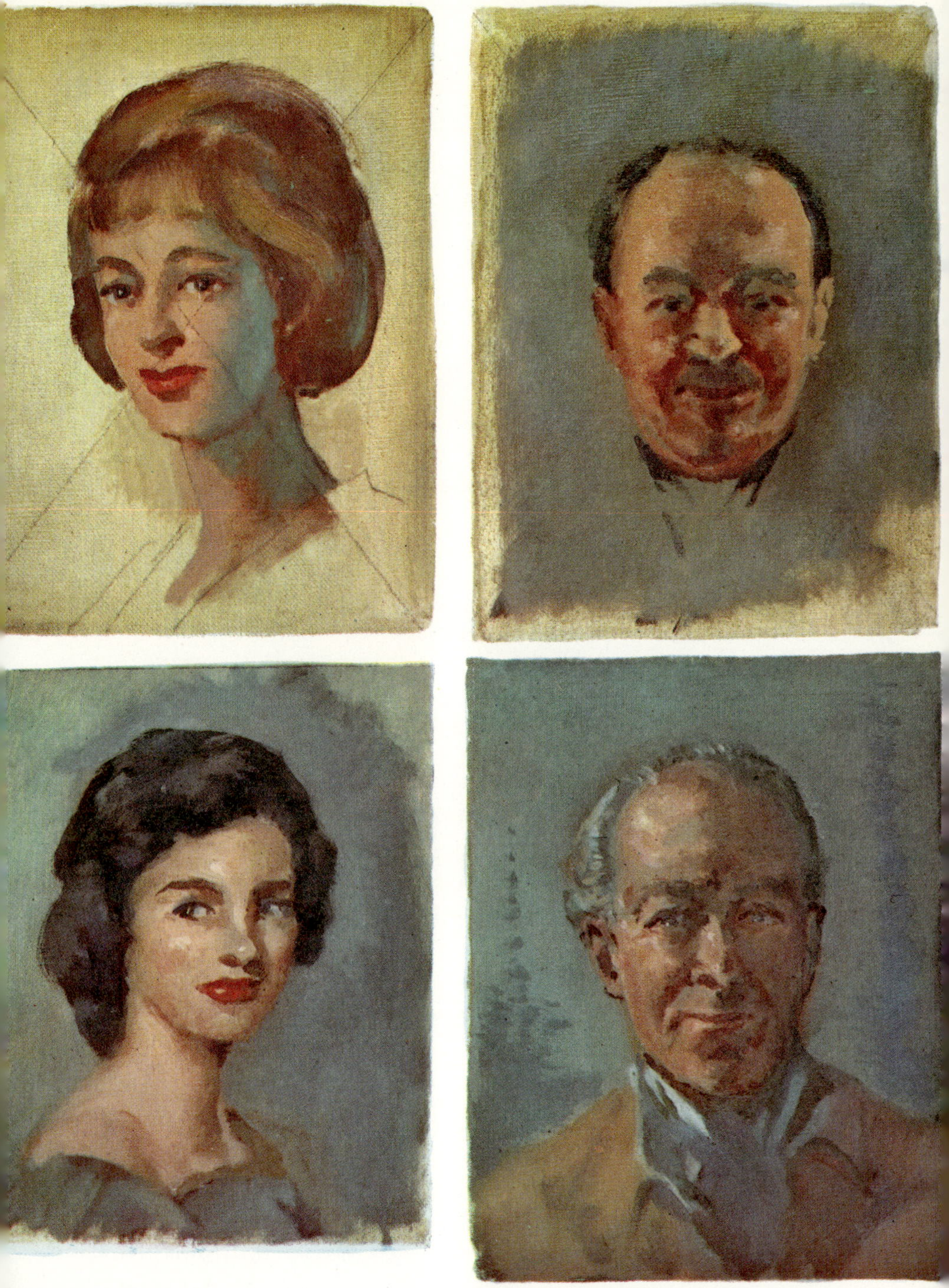

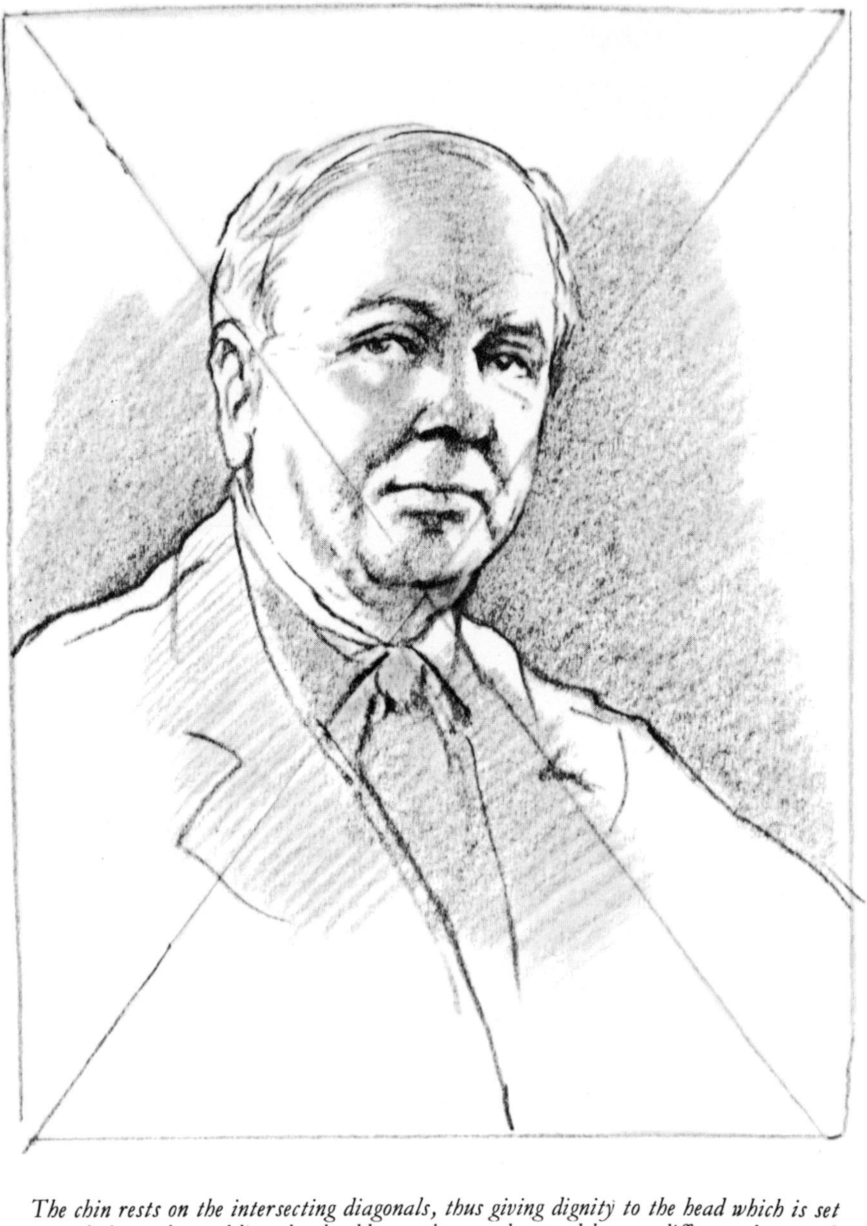

The chin rests on the intersecting diagonals, thus giving dignity to the head which is set at a slight angle, enabling the shoulders to have a slant and leave a different shape each side of the head.

furrows from the wings of the nostrils to the upper lip; all these surface markings except in old age, if too diligently followed, will only add years to your sitter—and the result will always be unflattering! A clean medium sized brush can be used to "brush" together two adjacent tints and soften the contours and blend the individual modelling of the features, especially round the mouth, and where the forehead retreats beneath the hair.

A little linseed oil can be mixed with your turps as the painting progresses. Make it a rule to load your light passages, i.e. forehead, nose and cheek bones and chin should be more solidly modelled in contrast to your shadow portions which should be kept relatively thin in texture. It is a good plan occasionally to place your easel close to your sitter so that you can compare the two heads together—stand well back to do this and half close your eyes if you are in doubt about tonal values.

As for size, 24″ by 20″ can give you room for a good sized head, and later on when confidence is gained a three-quarter length can be tried out on a 30″ by 25″ canvas or board.

After a number of sittings various portions of your painting may sink in and in contrast to more recent brushwork appear lacking in depth. Before working over these, oil them out with a clean brush and a little linseed. This will revive their original tone, which may then be seen to be the required strength.

When the surface of the painting has dried out but before the portrait is finished the pristine freshness of the colour all over can be restored by lightly rubbing it over with *retouché* varnish.

The *final Mastic* varnish should not be applied for at *least three months*. By that time the pigments underneath will be thoroughly dried out, and unless they are, a certain movement goes on and if sealed with varnish is liable to form little cracks on the surface.

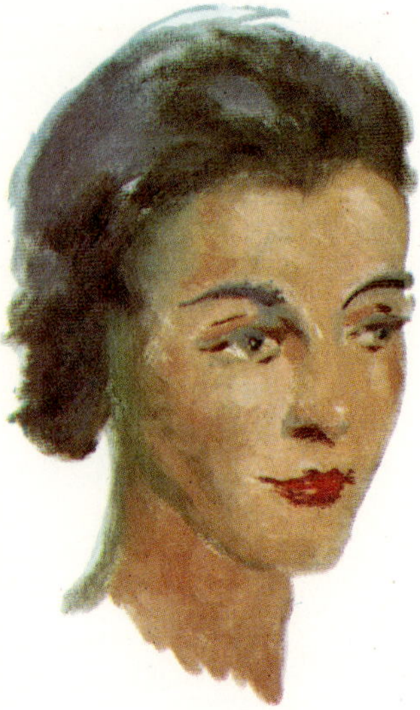
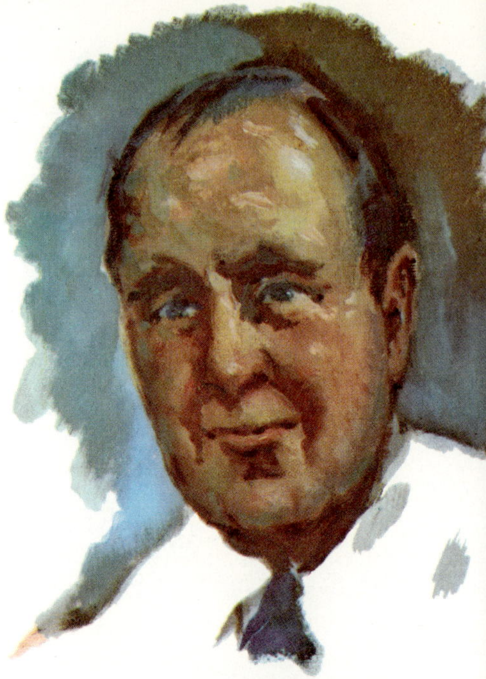
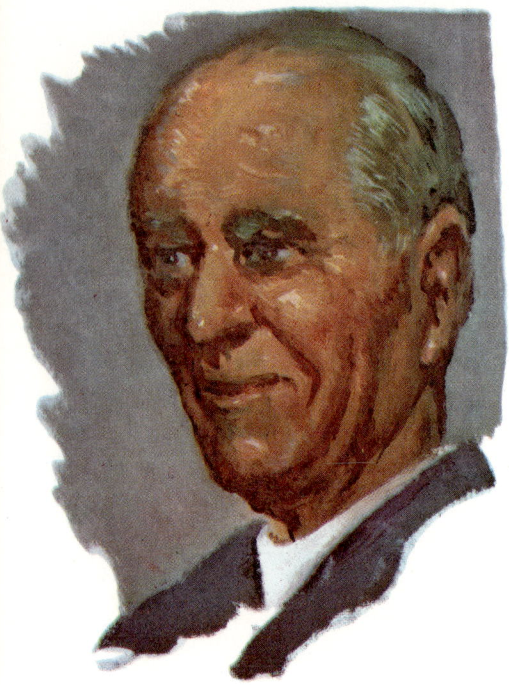
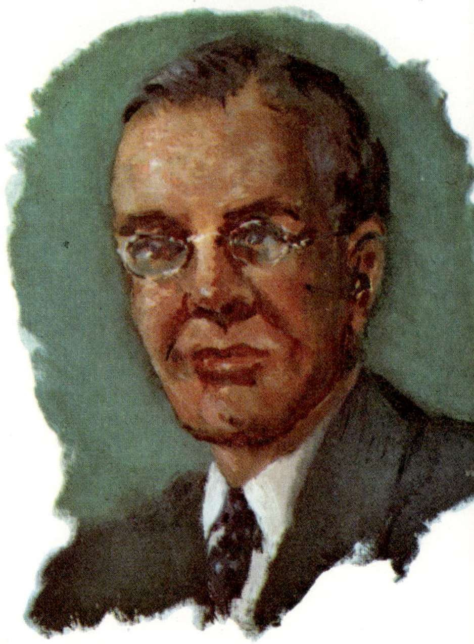

4 *Portraits—Stages and Sittings*

IT is idle to forecast the number of stages and sittings required to complete a painted head, especially if that implies one which not only satisfies the artist but his sitter as well.

Sometimes a happy spontaneous likeness can be brought about in a single sitting. A certain element of luck, or good fortune, must accompany the performance and when this co-ordination between the accurate eye and hand which selects the colours and controls the brush work occurs, a spirited sketch or the "premier coup" attack can often be counted a greater success than the portrait that is worked over many times and generally bears signs of labour.

It is a consoling thought however to realize that even professional painters of high standing have, on occasions, wrestled for many sittings and then confessed themselves beaten.

Augustus John has related in his reminiscences an occasional flying start that has become bogged down and rejected. And I remember a story of Cézanne when after countless sittings he could only report progress on the shirt front of his patient sitter!

Picasso's famous portrait of Miss Gertrude Stein also went through many tortuous vicissitudes and at the finish, if I remember rightly, the eyes were repainted from memory! As I am not primarily a painter of portraits I cannot share in these bad patches, but I can well sense the frustration which must accompany them. That missing "something" evades the painter who has then to resort to a repair job, and when this has to be undertaken, the trouble really starts.

Reginald Eves, whose portraits of men were so magnificently alive and unworried in technique, relied on this "premier coup" attack. From the word "go", he painted to finish and if the portrait did not "come", as we say, he would immediately scrap it and start on another.

Indeed he told me on one occasion he used up three reserve canvases before he struck lucky and "it came easily". "I had no trouble with it," is another frequent expression I have heard portrait painters use, which implies that sometimes they did!

Now a landscape as we have seen is rarely a "portrait" of the view, unless of course something topographic is required. Indeed it is the painter's expression, what he saw in the subject, that redeems the painting from being merely a factual statement.

In a portrait however a compromise is demanded. A likeness there must be but it should be removed from *photographic* accuracy, that is, the artist, like the landscapist, should superimpose his personal view of the sitter, i.e. How he or she looks *to him*. If at the same time (and this is where a measure of luck comes in) he can please himself, the sitter and, even more, the person who has commissioned the portrait, the painter can indeed be congratulated!

It may appear from the foregoing that I have a prejudice for the sketch as against the elaboration of the finished painting. I suppose I have in mind examples of the former which rank as high as any so-called finished work. The quick sketch of a person may well produce the closest likeness and be much nearer to real life than any elaborately finished picture.

"Here" (and I quote) "is one of the enigmas of painting which faces the artist as he works and has always faced the critic. In the work of some artists of the past such as Holbein and Ingres, preliminary sketches are so evidently only preparations

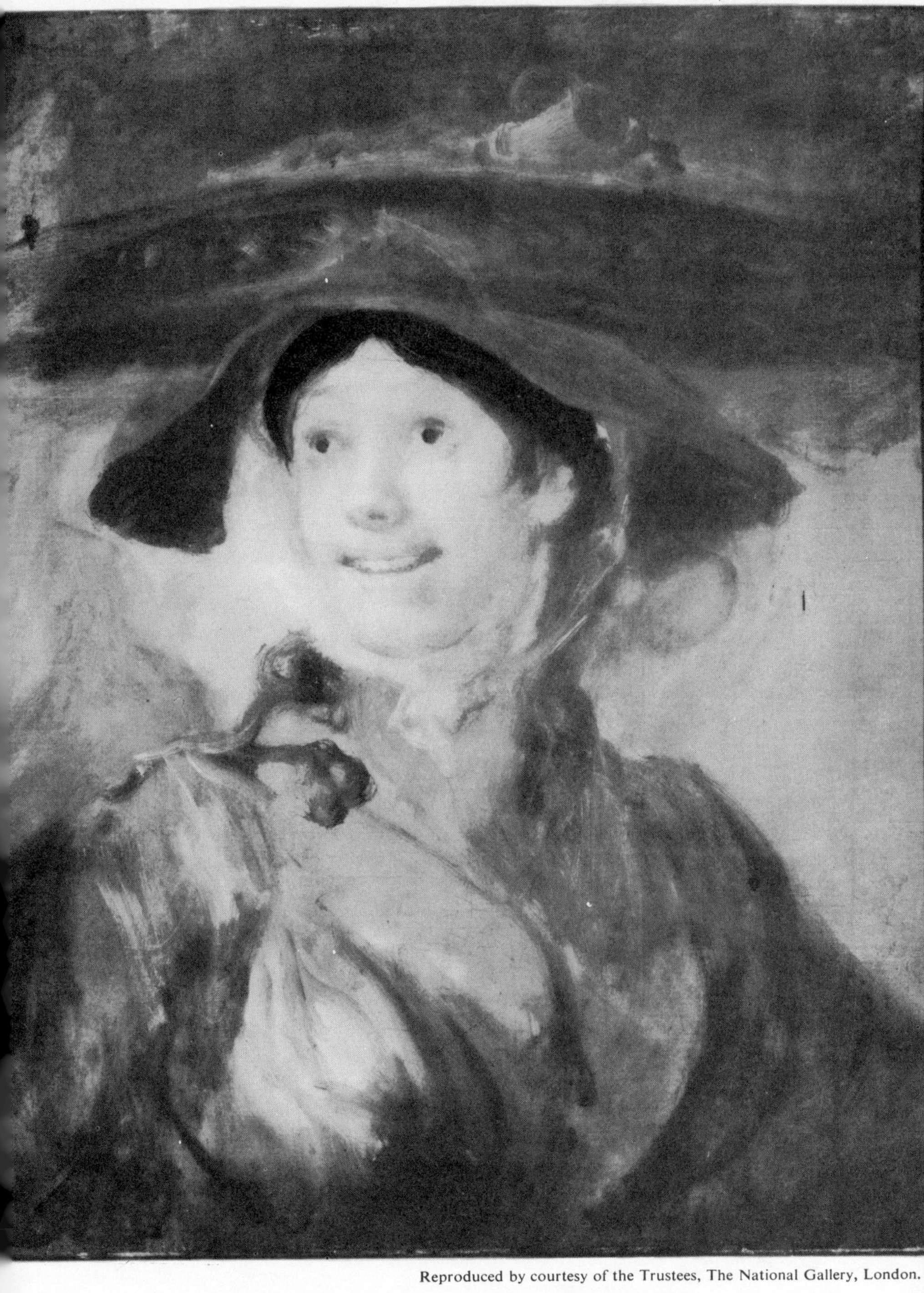

"The Shrimp Girl" by William Hogarth

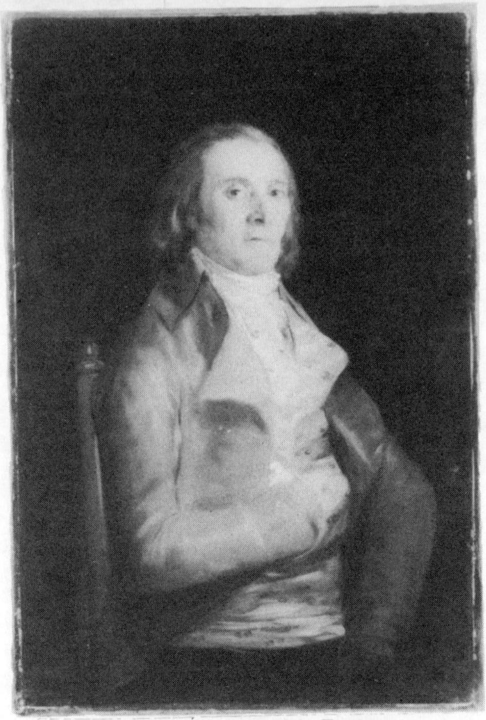

Reproduced by courtesy of the Trustees, The National Gallery, London.

"Dr Peral" by Goya

for the final achievement. But critics have often come to the conclusion that the sketch may both be the best likeness (if it is a portrait) and the best work of Art."

We have on record the famous "Shrimp Girl" by Hogarth, proof positive that the sketch or impression can outshine the completed portrait in vivacity and character—in this case unmatched in English Art, at any rate.

Vivacity is the word which aptly describes the appeal of many great portraits. Look at, or rather study, the features of Goya's famous portrait of Doctor Peral in our National Gallery. The mocking eyes, the disdainful lips which seem to hesitate between a smirk and a sneer—they are painted with an inspired gesture or flourish which can only be matched in the heads of Velasquez and in perhaps a minor degree in some of Gainsborough's women portraits—where the character lies in the pout or droop of the sitter's mouth just as much as in the melting or haughty look of the eyes. The so-called "life-like" portrait, far from deceiving anybody, only offends our eyes with the static stare of a waxwork. But the effortless result is of course the reward for the numerous studies where many signs of labour mark our honest progress. Perhaps "make haste slowly" should be our safest watchword.

5 *Lighting*

LIGHTING can be of immeasurable assistance when drawing and especially when painting heads. Indeed without due attention as to how the face is lit—and that implies the best way of lighting the *particular* head—a failure or a "near miss" is almost a foregone conclusion. Lighting from one side or the other can subdue or accentuate features in a marked degree—and the stronger the light, the stronger the modelling. Let us take a few examples and see how lighting affects the features.

If the head is directly facing the light, there will be very little shadow forms to help us with the modelling of the nose, especially if it is a full face. If however the face is lit from above, then shadows will occur under the brows, under the nose and under the chin, in accordance with the projection of the features. A prominent nose will throw a stronger cast shadow than a small childish nose or one that is tip-tilted.

For general purposes then, it is advisable to light the head from the *side* and to vary the strength of the lighting by placing the sitter near to the window—or some distance away and if needs be screening the light by the adjustment of curtains. Some faces demand strong shadow forms, others require less dramatic contrast, to reveal character. But only care in lighting will demonstrate how the best results can be obtained.

And in this art of lighting, the camera (for all I have said against it) has shown us what can be done by experiment—in

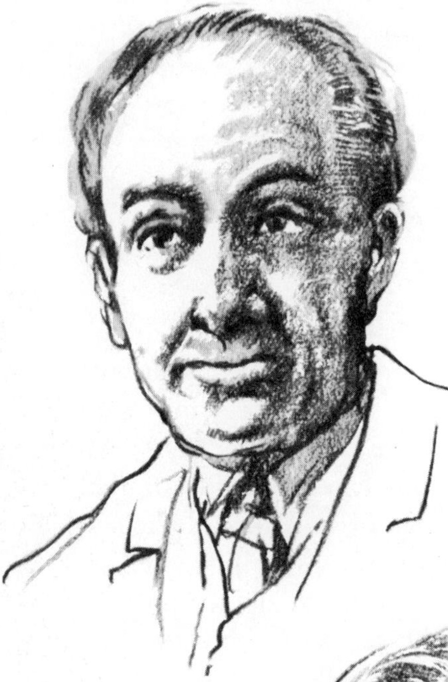

1. *Top lighting from left.*

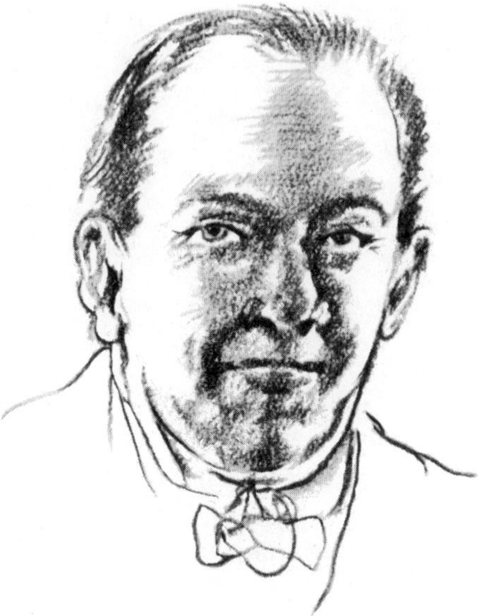

2. *Strong light from both sides.*

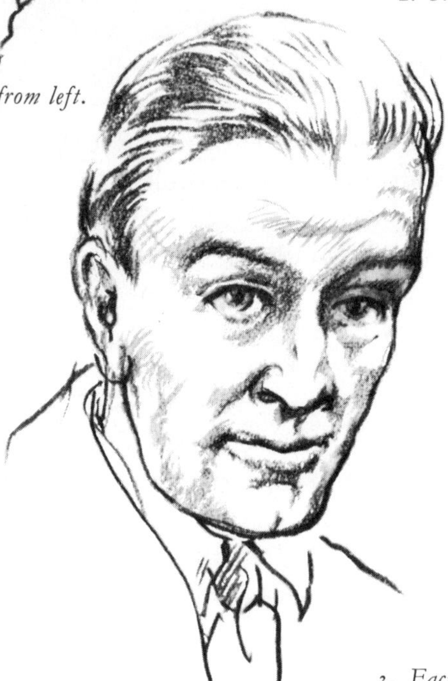

3. *Facing the light.*

"*An Old Man as S. Paul*"
by Rembrandt

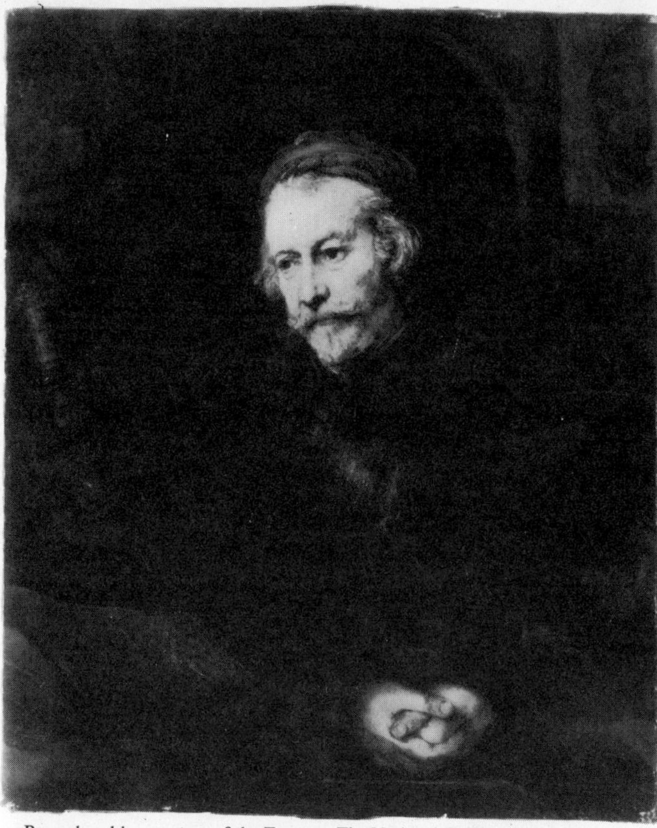

Reproduced by courtesy of the Trustees, The National Gallery, London.

particular, lighting both sides of the head and what one could term "flood lighting" where the origin of light comes up from below and pin points high lights of features and contours which hitherto have been relegated to half tones.

This Art of chiaroscuro (light and shade) was first developed by Rembrandt (the spot light in surrounding gloom) with great effect, noticeably in his portraits of old age, where the face was illuminated by a single shaft of light from a window high up behind the painter's back.

It has now been developed further and can come to our aid in many cases where character is often achieved by throwing the features of the sitter into sharp relief. But, and this must be said, obsession with lighting effects for *effect* can only result in a "gimmick". Better far to recall some of Whistler's famous portraits, that of his mother, Thomas Carlyle and the enchanting

"Lillie in our alley", where any such lighting aids as those I have been discussing are completely absent. These portraits are seen in such an evenly distributed illumination that no cast shadows exist! These people he painted with such naturalistic charm could be said to live in a two dimensional world of their own, where time stood still, and shadows never encroached to disturb their serenity, but when depicted with such masterly regard for tone and knowledge of pattern are readily accepted and found completely satisfying as living portraits.

Another great portrait painter, Amadeo Modigliani, never modelled his sitter's features by light and shade, but relied on tone and a sensitive containing line to render solidity to the head.

Van Gogh made use of brushwork, changing the direction of his brush strokes to reveal the varied planes of the head and face. It would therefore be wise to repeat the warning that lighting is only justifiable if it reinforces the delineation of the features, for purposes of revealing character.

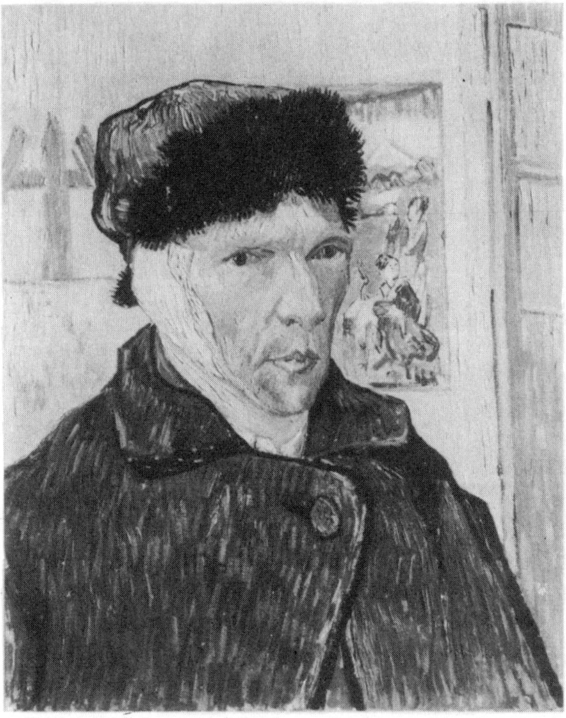

"Self-portrait, with bandaged ear" by Van Gogh

Reproduced by courtesy of the Courtauld Institute of Art, London.

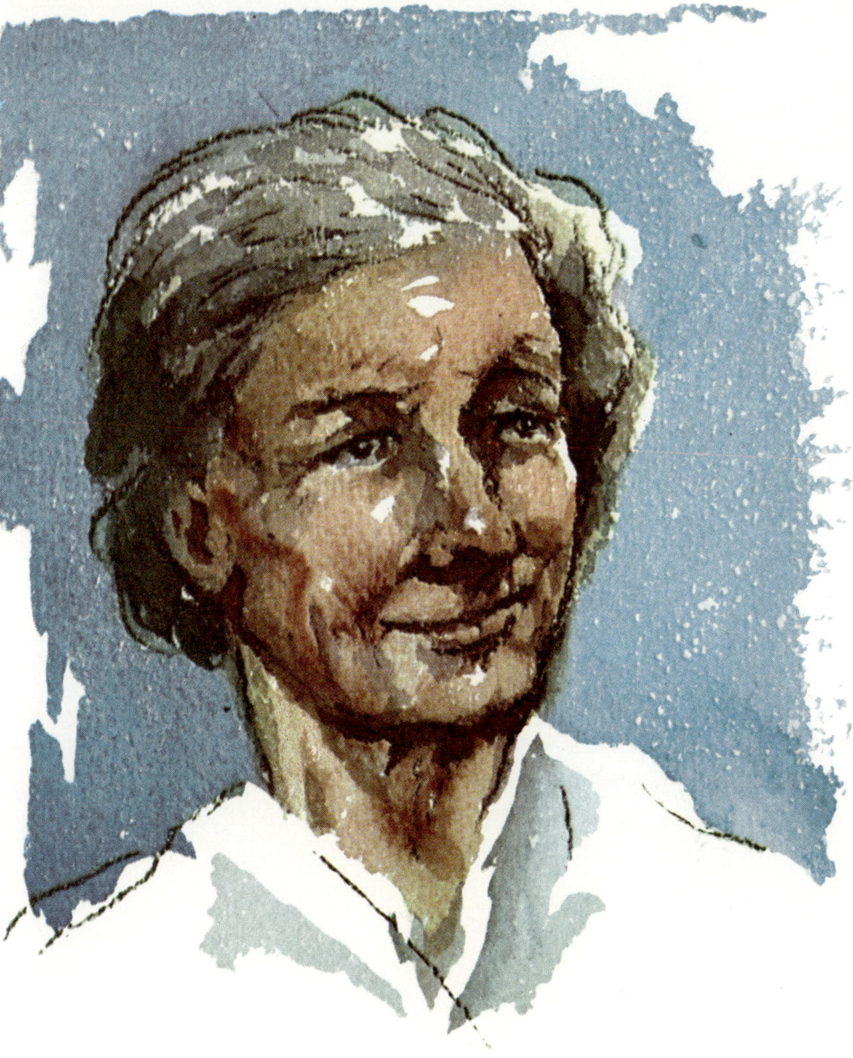

Pure watercolour. Highlights left.

6 *Heads in Watercolour*

THE medium of watercolour for portraits is always, to me, a doubtful performance. It has changed considerably and now offers a number of different techniques (which is fortunate for those who are unable to master the pure transparent method which was the traditionally accepted one up to about 1930). This subsequent technical freedom was a logical breakaway from the dry stippled method by which a head was modelled—like an enlarged miniature painting, a tedious performance to our eyes now—which produced a result in which everything was sacrificed to a high finish. The polished texture thus achieved robbed the face of both character and life. The looser and freer handling which followed went however to the other extreme. Dexterity in technique became the aim and certainly a portrait in watercolour when I was a student was a very skilled accomplishment, especially if a likeness matched up to the expert performance, as I believe it often did! Now we have however the offer of gouache —which is very similar in technique to an oil, except that the pigments are diluted with water instead of turps—or linseed oil (see chapter 3). There is also a middle-of-the-road method which combines a strong line drawing in pencil, chalk, or pen as a basis for transparent colour, and when these washes of colour are used merely to enhance the drawing rather than to complete the modelling, this technique is known as a tinted drawing. Then there is the drawing executed on a tinted paper,

Carbon drawing on grey tinted paper, heightened with white chalk.

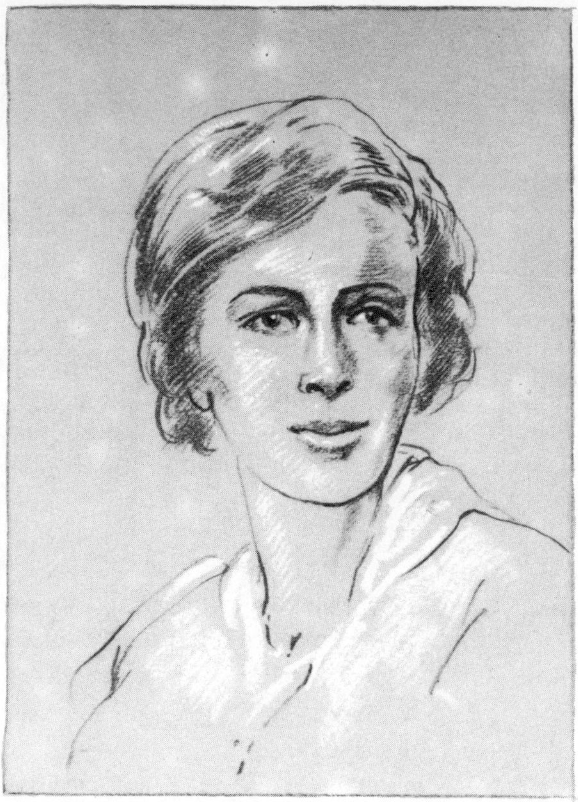

grey, buff or yellow and heightened with Chinese White. Finally there is pastel—a very popular medium for child portraits, but which can be dangerously pretty when tinted paper is used.

The difference between pastel and other mediums is that colour mixing is not necessary as all the required shades and tints are supplied by the pastels themselves. For example green is worked over blue, red over yellow, green over brown, on the paper itself, to obtain the tint or tone required. These in turn can be blended by rubbing them down or together with a soft rag or with your fingers.

It is obvious that in all these mediums the drawing is as important as the colouring, and this being accepted, the painting or colouring is a matter of personal preference and of necessity—a matter of trial and error.

Yellow Ochre wash over a chalk drawing (fixed) with high lights added with white.

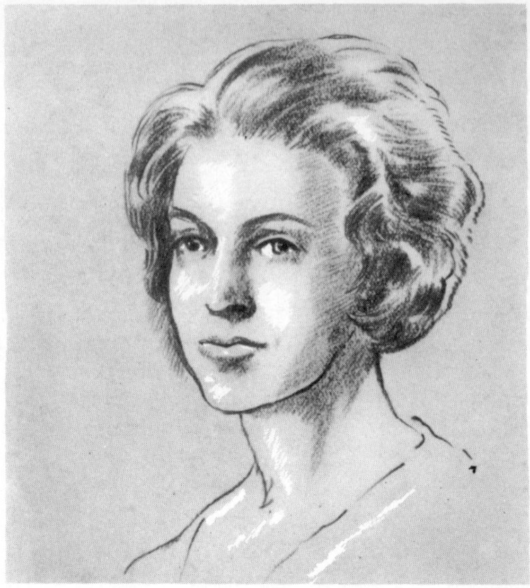

Experiments in watercolour, of which I have shown some examples, can be made by damping the area of the head first and applying the flesh tint all over the face before the surface of the paper dries. Or by washing in the shadow forms on a damp surface first and painting in the flesh tints over them before the previous shadows are *quite dry*, so that the edges are softened.

High lights can be lifted—with a stiffish brush and *clean* water—or superimposed afterwards with deft touches of Chinese White. In all cases, as with oil painting, accents either with a small brush or a pointed chalk (in which case the painting must be quite *dry*) should only be introduced in the last stages of the painting.

Backgrounds should always be painted in a suggestive manner, simple and cool in colour. Keep reds or browns out of your colour scheme and eschew a detailed design.

Your palette, as in oils (see following chapter), should be restricted in numbers and the same range of colours can be equally well applied, with the exception of green. Viridian will replace Terra Vert. Payne's Grey can be used in the place of Ivory Black and Vandyck Brown may take the place of Burnt Umber.

But again the final choice of colours must be an individual one.

The Palette for Oils

Let me say at the outset that in portrait painting, or more especially in the terms of this book, painting faces—which does not sound so professional—the fewer colours you use, the better. This is not for economical reasons, but common sense. The temptation to call upon a number of separate colours instead of achieving the tint, shade or tone which is desired by mixing the colours from your pre-selected list is—or appears to be—irresistible, but must be resisted. Experiment by all means with different ranges of colour, because in the end the final choice must be yours, but whatever the range limit yourself to the essential colours. Every artist is found to favour certain pigments and decry others, and their choice may happen to coincide with yours. With this in mind I would suggest (rather than dictate) for a start, that the reader will not go far wrong if he obtains the following paints as a *safe* palette:

1 Flake White
2 Yellow Ochre
3 Light Red
4 Vermilion
5 Terra Vert
6 Cobalt Blue
7 Ivory Black
8 Alizarin Crimson

(Burnt Umber, Lemon Chrome and Ultramarine Blue can be brought in as reserves.)

Of course, individual local colour can and often d
important part in obtaining the authentic personal
bucolic or rustic type, the dusky, sunburnt or native
florid or pallid face. These may need an additio
included in my list. For normal complexions, howev
palette which I have given will with judicious mixin
requirements. Given good modelling and accurate
the painting will achieve that harmony which is depe
few colours. A glance at many of the Old Master port
especially of the Dutch and Italian Schools, will prove this.

Even in the portrayal of old age, colouration and texture of the skin must not be inspected too closely, as Rembrandt has clearly demonstrated in his masterly portraits of wrinkled maturity.

Ivory Black by itself should never be used for shadows and accents. This often happens when the beginner paints from photographs, where the black and white print always exaggerates the tone contrasts. If these are followed literally, the origin of your painting will at once be shown up. I will allude to this again.

However dark—or black—the hair may be, a mixture of crimson and blue with a touch of brown or green will be seen to suffice for the strength of tone required. Black should only be used with other colours to subdue, degrade or mute the tint. Indeed to give depth and quality a *touch* of black with all your colours can achieve this end and prevent a "pretty" or chalky effect, which must be avoided at all costs.

8 *The Painter and the Camera*

FOR some years now photography has played an increasing part in portrait painting. This, I think, is a pity, if not a positive danger, especially to the student. To some the camera takes precedence over the unaided skill of the young artist who has learnt to lean almost entirely on its mechanical eye. With professional's it is not uncommon to hear of a sitter being photographed first and the choice of position and expression fixed upon before the painting begins, and much preliminary work even then is based on the photograph before the first sitting is arranged.

In some extreme (one hopes) cases, the chosen print is enlarged, squared up and even developed on a sensitized canvas before the painter starts work.

To the purist this "prefabricated" portrait is anathema and for my part I would prefer a colour photograph and be done with it!

The temptation often arises when the amateur is weak on drawing or where a painter who having built up a reputation for a particular aspect of Art suddenly takes up portraiture as a change or for financial gain.

Whether such portraits that are painted from photographs lose their integrity in contrast to the long practice and experience of their author's former work is an open question; certainly one of these painters has openly acknowledged his debt to the camera (Walter Sickert went so far as to sign his name under that of the photographer on his picture of Gwen ffrangcon-Davies in the

Tate Gallery). I would of course add a rider to the effect that if properly used and kept under control by the *professional* painter, the photograph can be accepted as a basic aid *on which to build up a personal statement*. In the hands of a student or beginner however, it should be viewed as a dangerous ally, a spurious friend who can let you down badly. It is a short cut as any slavish copying must be.

It should be realized that in the halcyon days of *great* portraiture the magic was in the eye and hand of the painter alone—his integrity remained unquestioned until the advent of the camera.

For this reason anybody who desires a real knowledge of the work of the great portrait painters will fail to find but a few examples in our contemporary exhibitions, but should turn his steps towards the National, the Tate, the Wallace and Dulwich College Galleries, for it is on their walls that the craft in its purest form will be found.

Only in the case of a posthumous portrait, I should say, can a photograph be said to be absolutely indispensable!

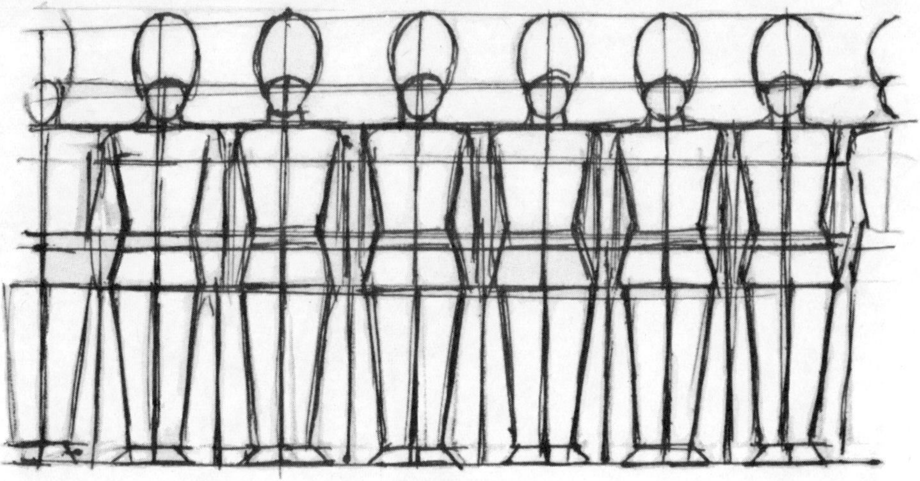

In company.

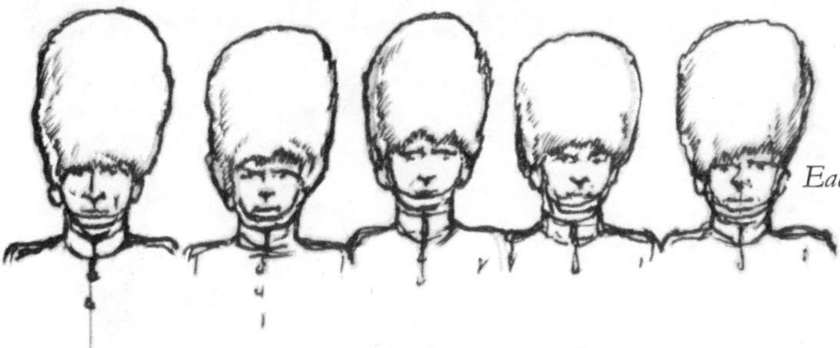

Each an individual.

9 *Figure Drawing*

FIGURE drawing, or drawing people, if you like, brings us literally face to face with humanity. And models are never in short supply. Young and old, men and women, boys and girls (and babies) confront us at every turn. And like their faces, their bodies are all different. Even (in an extreme case) in a perfect alignment of soldiers on parade. Ask any inspecting officer as he goes slowly down the ranks, and he will tell you that although they are all dressed the same, each looking steadfastly ahead, with shoulders back, head erect and legs together and at a distance exactly resemble a line of static robots, when inspected one by one and at close quarters, these men remain individuals, each proclaiming himself different from his neighbour (see illustration).

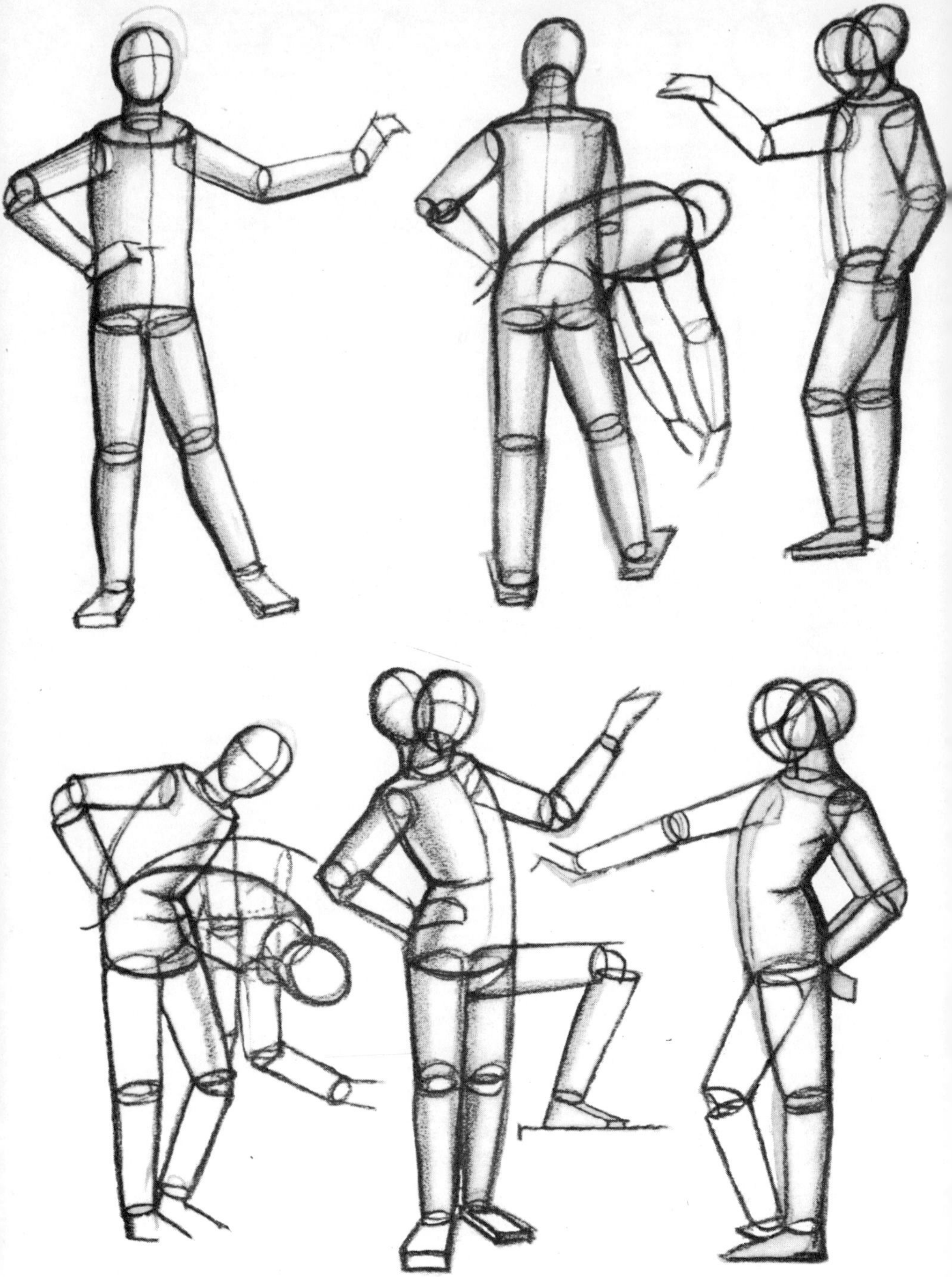

The tubular figure.

Trunk can bend in its own length—forwards—sideways (limited degree) and backwards (limited extent).

And so it is and far more obvious when "off parade" we go about our normal jobs. Not only are we all different but whatever position we take, it is *our own* particular way of standing and our way of sitting. Whether relaxed or in action we all *perform* differently—however slightly it may be—and this leads us to the first of our problems in drawing figures.

The people we draw (or paint) must move and behave *naturally*. Normally we have our bodies under our control. We do nothing by numbers, we sit at ease, we stand without effort, we walk, run or jump rhythmically. And once the body is in action, we must depict the movements as they are performed by human beings and not as puppets or automatons.

In order to achieve this rhythm of line, we must study closely and watch what happens not only in the head or arms and legs, but how they all work together. And that's not easy! But it is surprising once we have learnt to use our eyes in this way, what they can take in and with practice retain so that we keep a mental, if not physical, image before us when we are actually at work.

Equally important is the realization that inside the outer covering of clothes is the *solid rounded* cylindrical body. It is over these tubular forms that our clothes hang (in folds) or cling or are stretched, according to the material and the size and shape we are!

And it is in these folds, wrinkles and creases that the necessary clues are to be found.

Throw a sheet over a chair, hang it up on a hook, spread it over a table, drape it over somebody's shoulders and each time the material will behave or adapt itself differently, *according to the surface form it covers.*

The trouble is that so often the drawing of a coat on the body of a person looks as if it were hung on a clothes line, with nothing underneath!

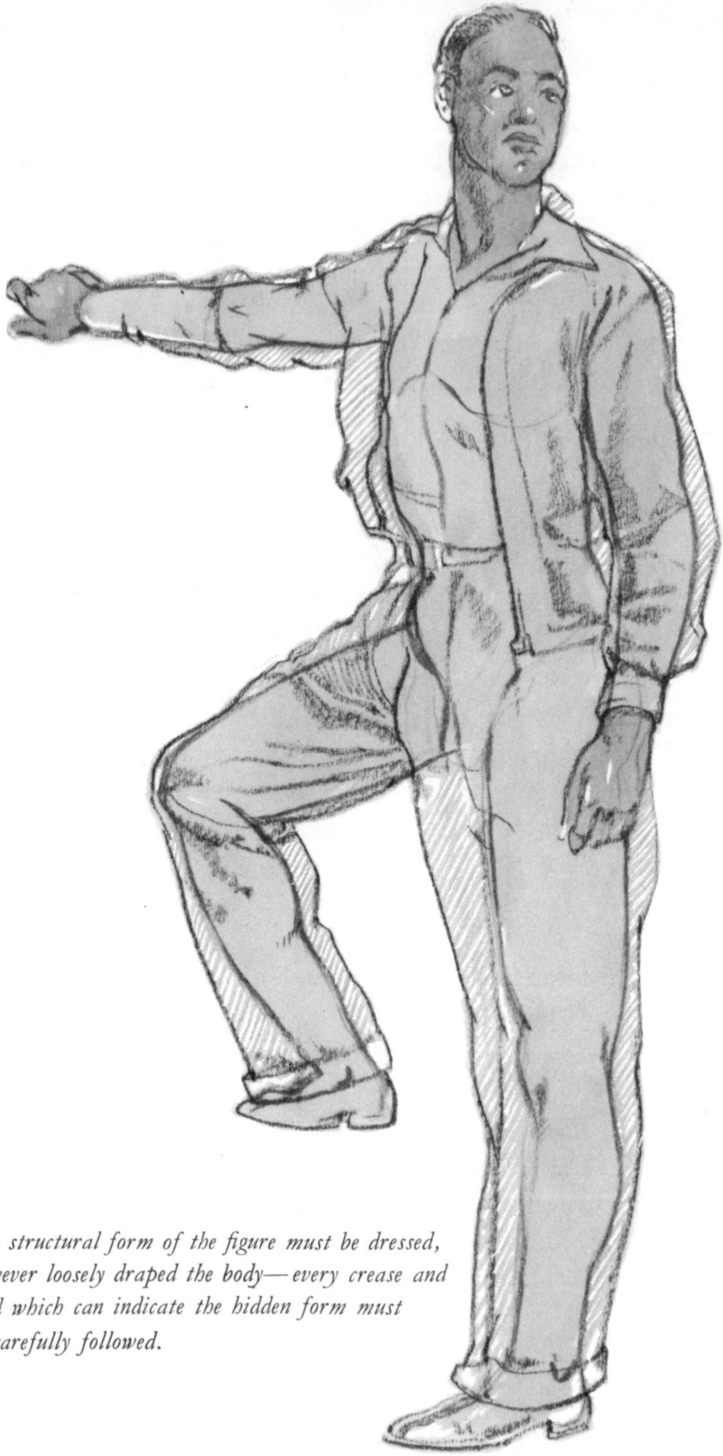

The structural form of the figure must be dressed, however loosely draped the body—every crease and fold which can indicate the hidden form must be carefully followed.

Thus, it is most important to remember what does function beneath and I hope that the illustrations I have chosen will make it doubly sure. It is for this reason that there are so many of them and that the captions are kept short and sweet, as in my experience demonstration is easier to follow than any amount of painstaking description.

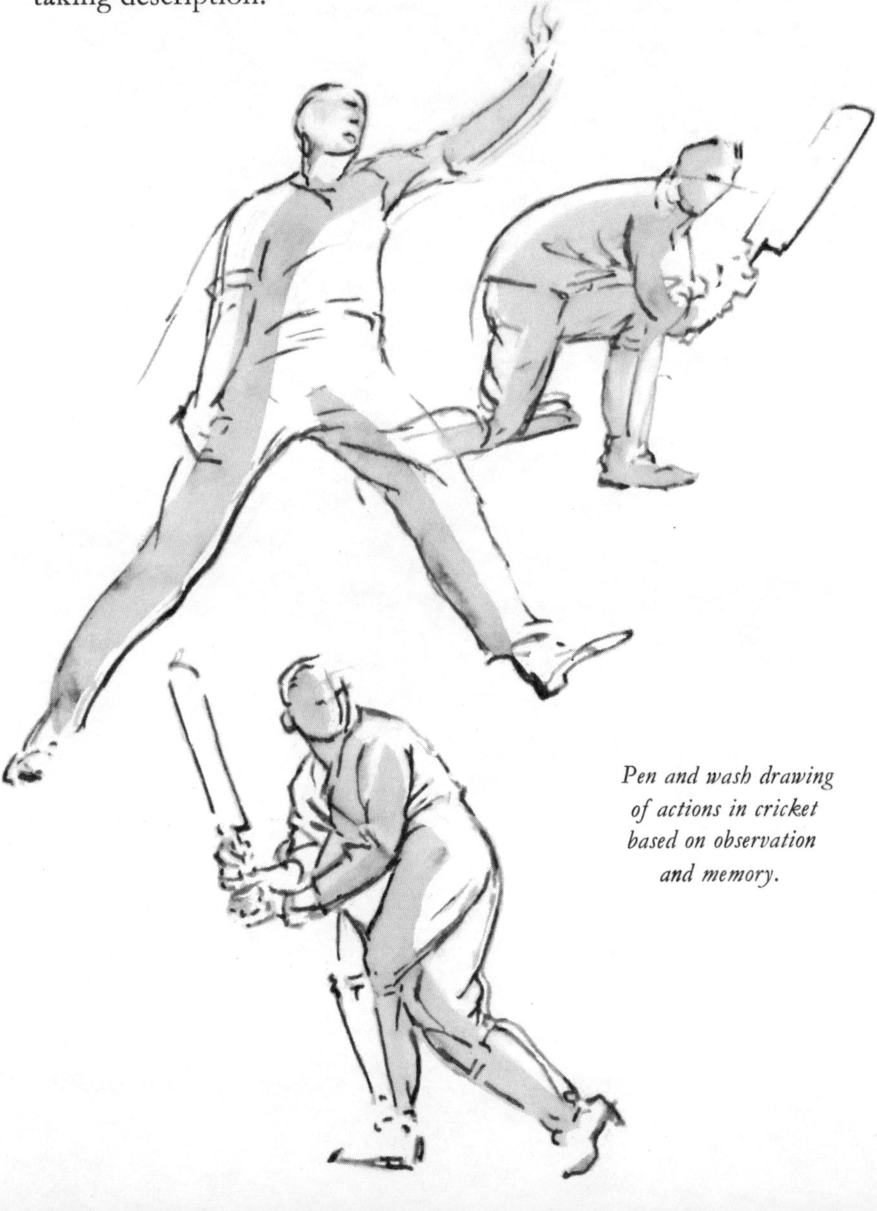

Pen and wash drawing of actions in cricket based on observation and memory.

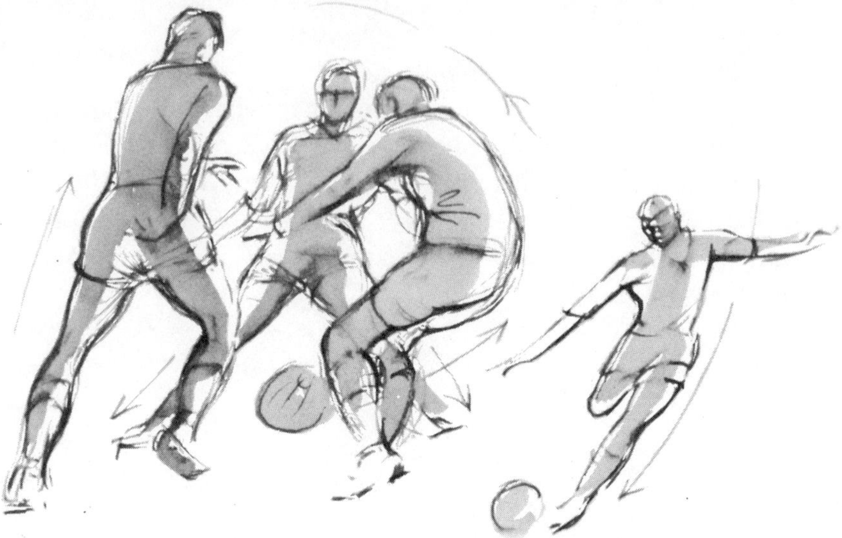

Pen and wash drawing of actions in football based on observation and memory.

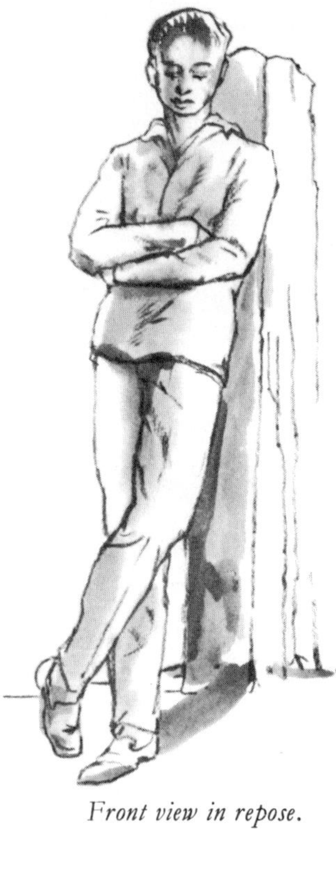

Front view in repose.

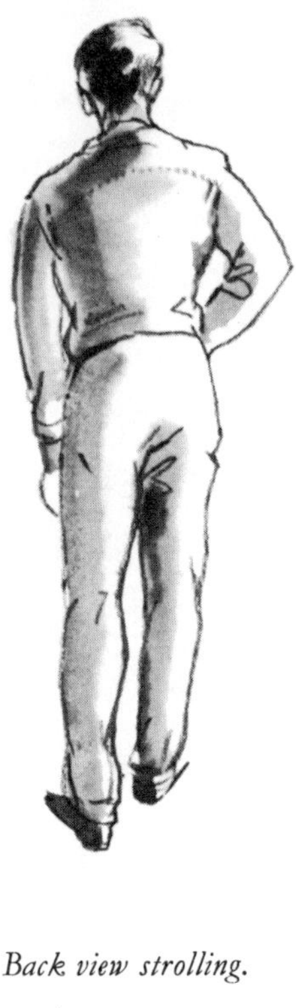

Back view strolling.

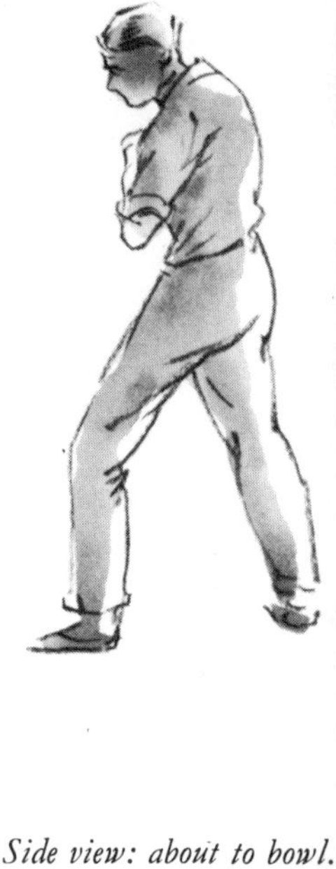

Side view: about to bowl.

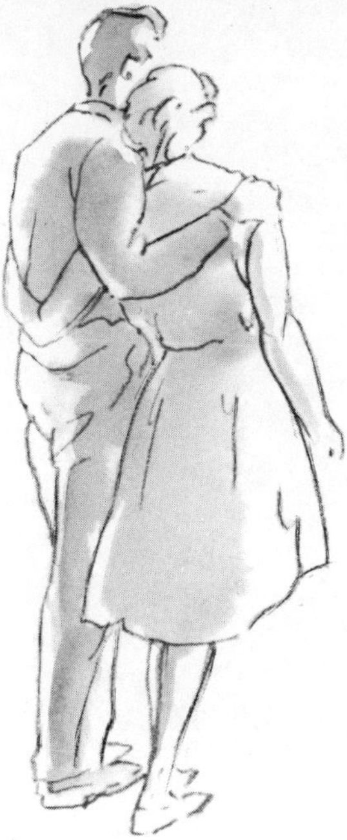

The new moon.

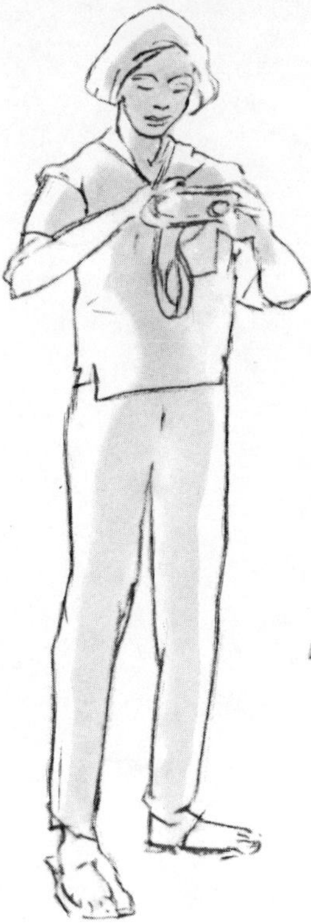

The new camera.

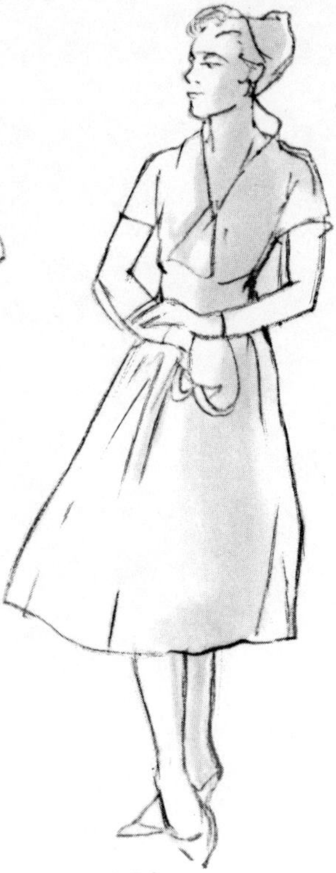

The new dress.

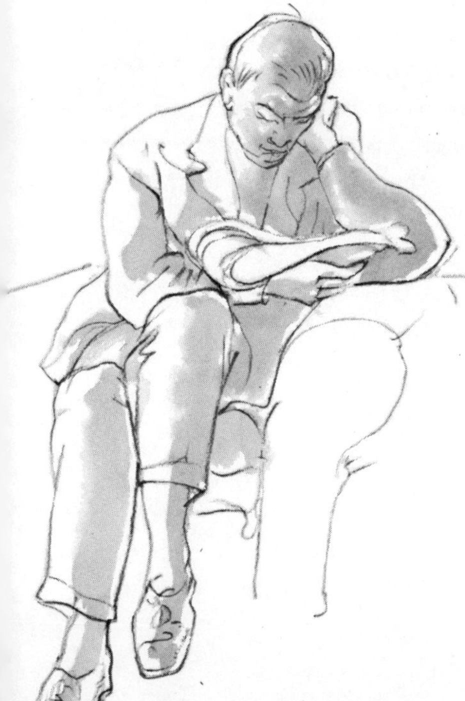

Sitting reading—his position.

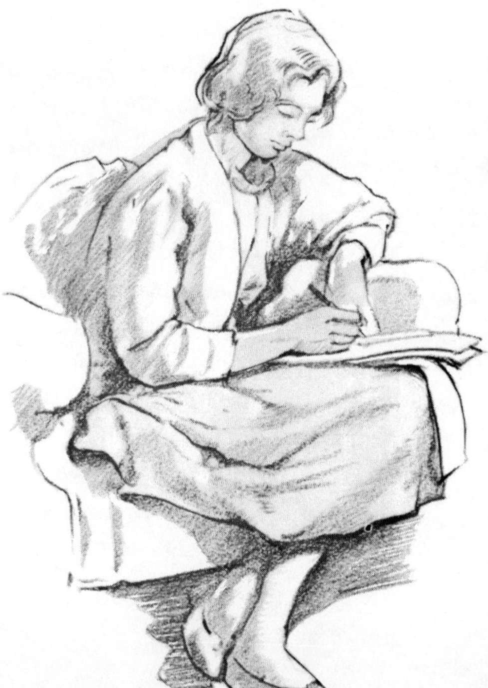

Sitting writing—her position.

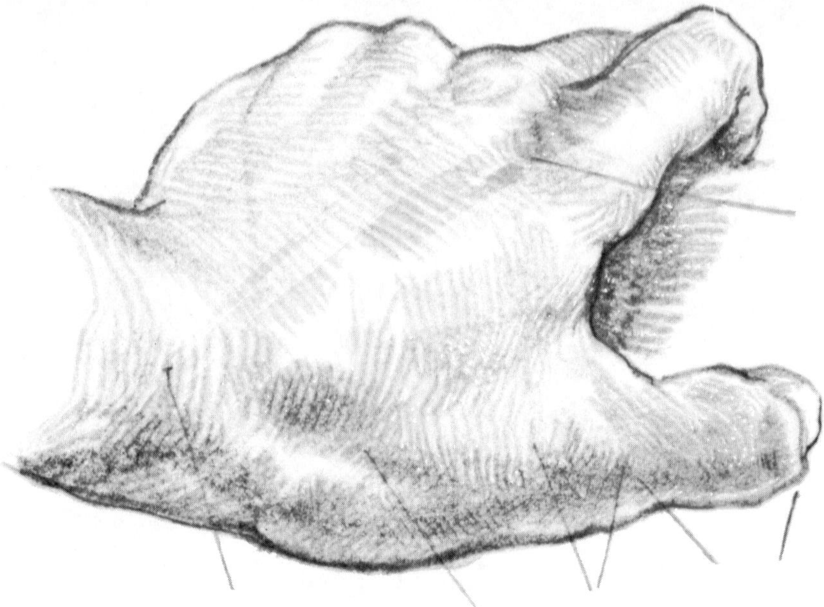

PRELIMINARY STUDIES

All down the ages, it is through the life studies of the Old Masters that we appreciate and value their finished works. For in their drawings they proclaim their mastery over the tools of their trade. In them we not only see what they are striving for, but can actually follow their train of thought and sense the drawing hand, sometimes bold, sometimes tentative, sometimes even a trifle "off the beat", but in the main following with great accuracy and confidence what is required to evoke the right image, character or action in question.

There is nothing so spontaneous as the graphic line, because nothing comes between the drawing hand and the paper, except the pen, pencil or chalk (and only perhaps an inch of that!). And to see just how descriptive this line can be, we have only to study the drawings of Michelangelo, Leonardo da Vinci, Rembrandt, Ingres or Watteau, to name only a few of the great draughtsmen, who each in his way, with exquisite sensitivity, tremendous gusto, or that nervous notation born of long experience, can form in a few strokes, an expression of age, innocence, serenity,

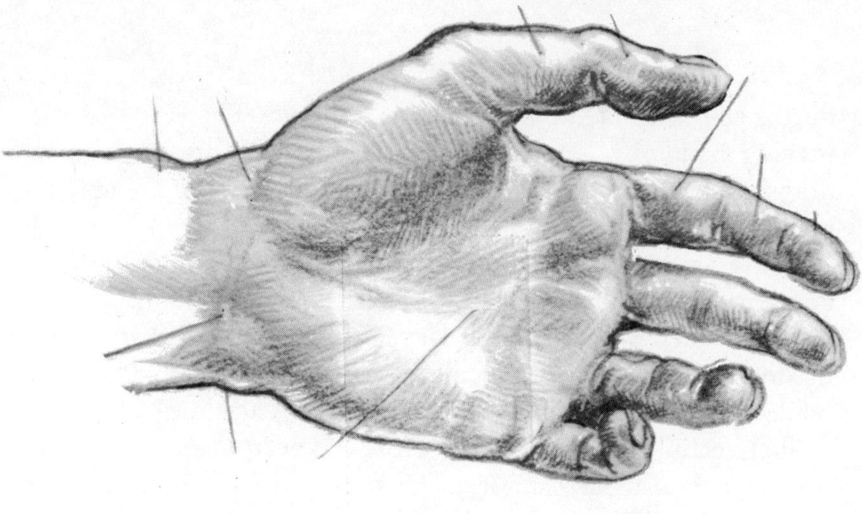

Separate studies of hands showing the variety of shapes dependent on the movement of the fingers in action.

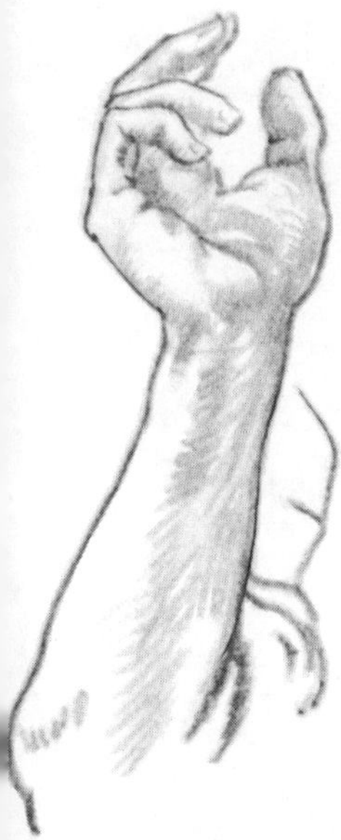

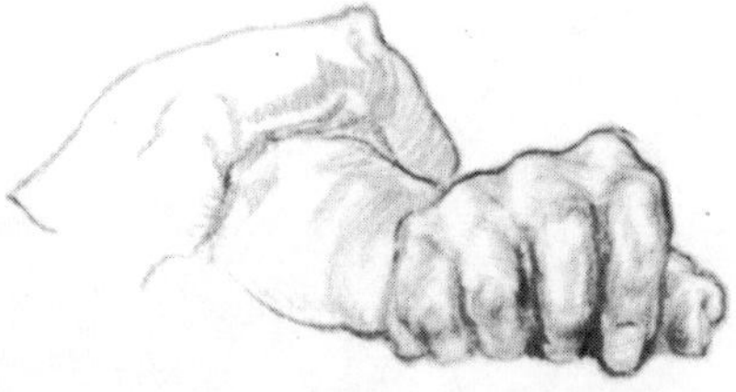

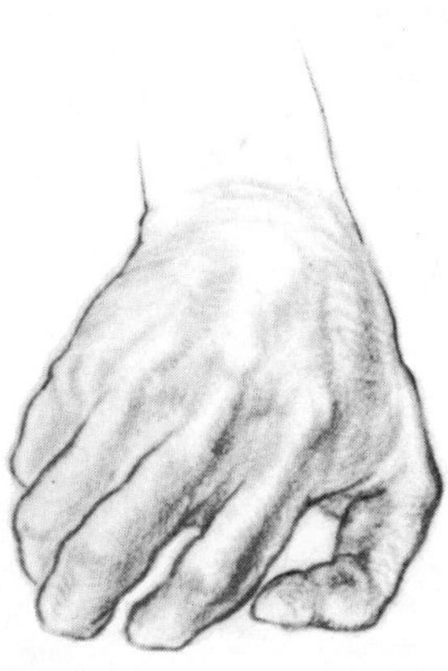

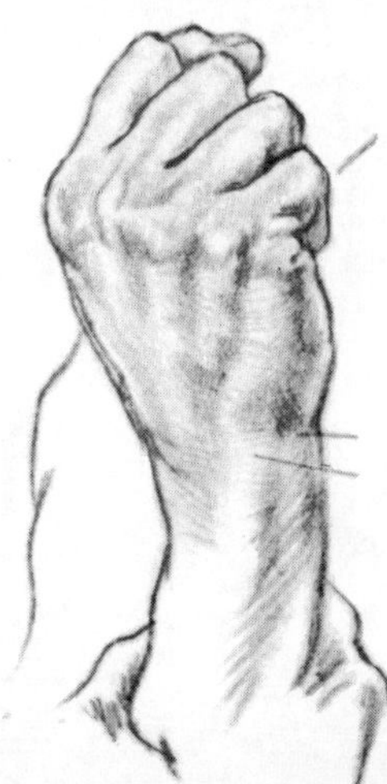

mirth, alarm, grief, nobility, cruelty or love. The study of the praying hands by Dürer, for example, is not only a lesson in drawing, but in the act of worship, for in them we are able to picture the whole figure in an act of devotion.

It will always be found however that in these studies there is far more than impeccable accuracy. It is a subtle addition, the lack of which shows up the clever drawing from that of the master draughtsman. For while the first excites our envy for a while, the second commands our respect for all time.

Slick technique always wilts before the necromancy of a great drawing. And if we cannot all be so gifted we can at least set about our studies with humility, though it means mounting the ladder rung by rung. By learning the slow way, it will enable us to approach more nearly to our ideal.

Some of these "approaches" I have culled from my own sketch books. If they are found to be far from the ideal they are put in "the witness box" to support the "rung by rung" approach!

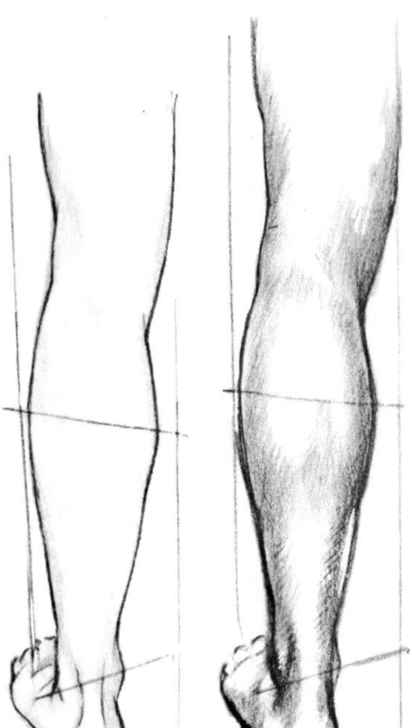

Left: Outline of male left leg.
Right: Form of male left leg.

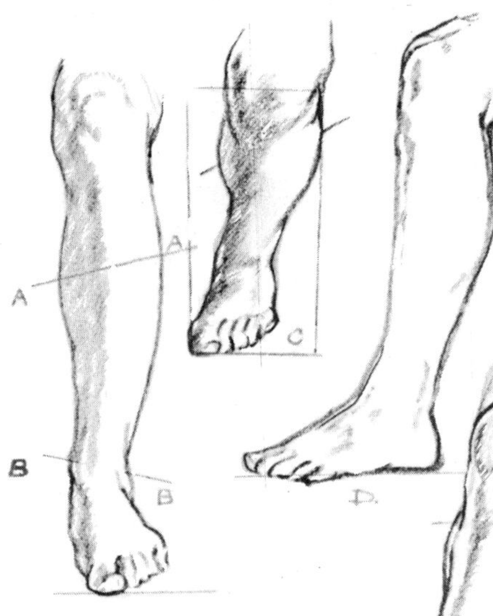

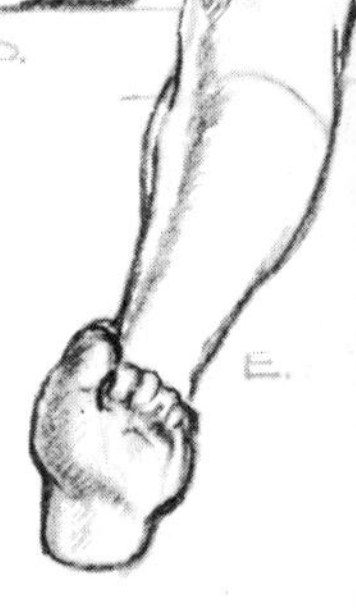

A The calf is higher on the outside.
B The outer ankle is lower than the inside one.
C Foreshortened leg.
D The great toe is on the inside.
E Foreshortened raised foot.

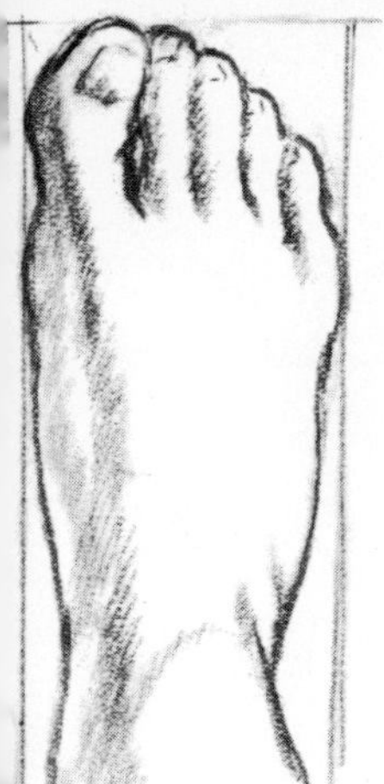

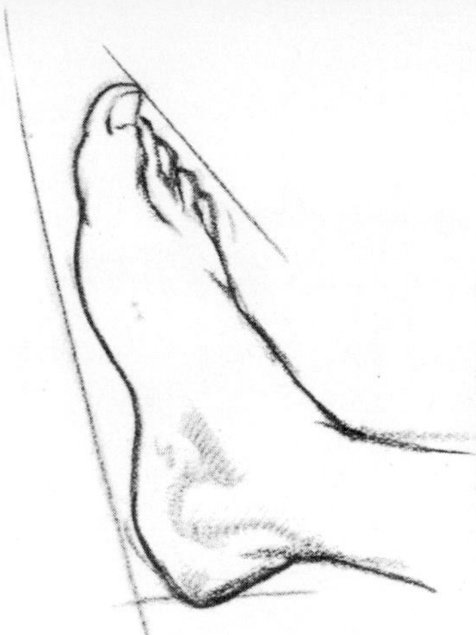

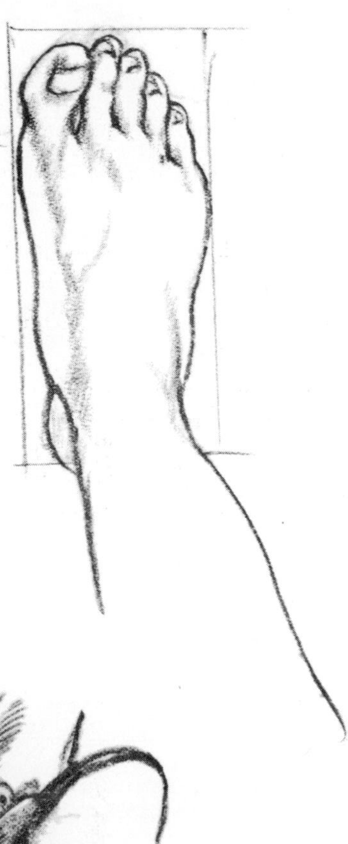

In comparison with the fingers of the hand, the toes act in unison with the direction of the foot.

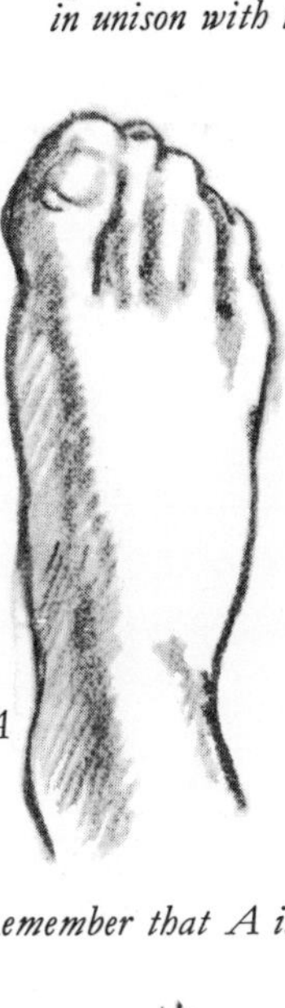

A

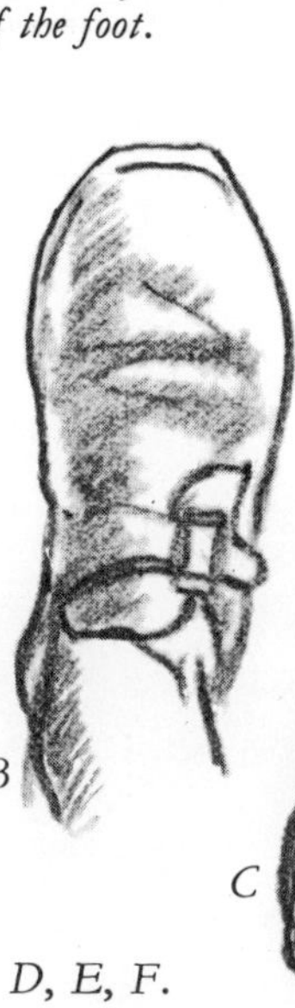

B

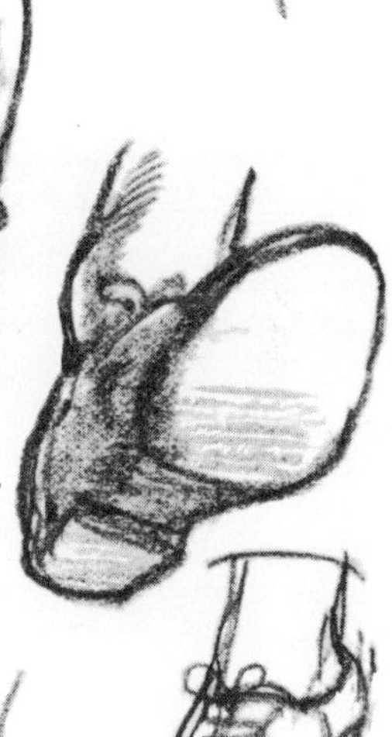

C

Remember that A is inside B, *C*, *D*, *E*, F.

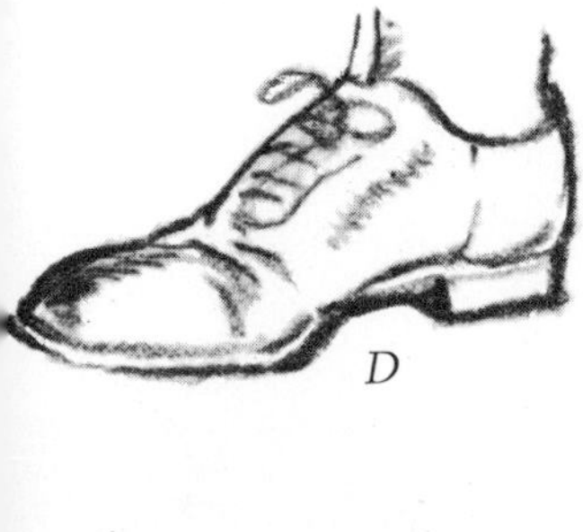

D

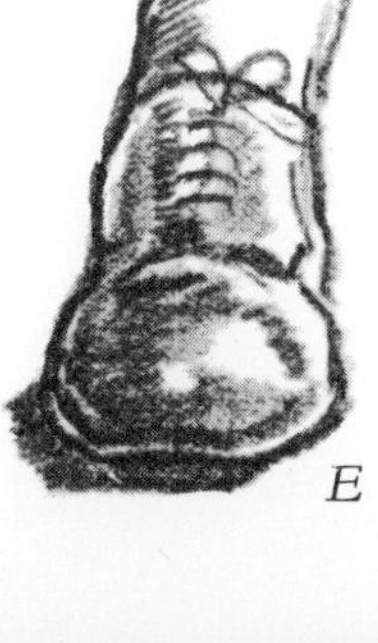

E

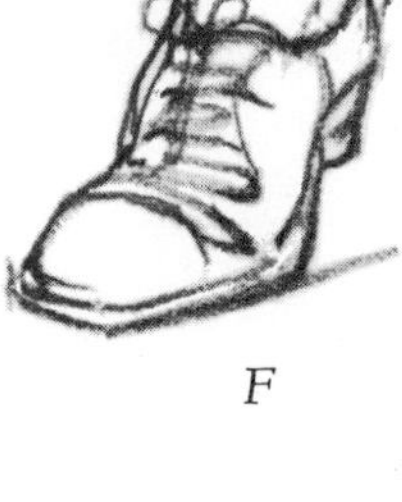

F

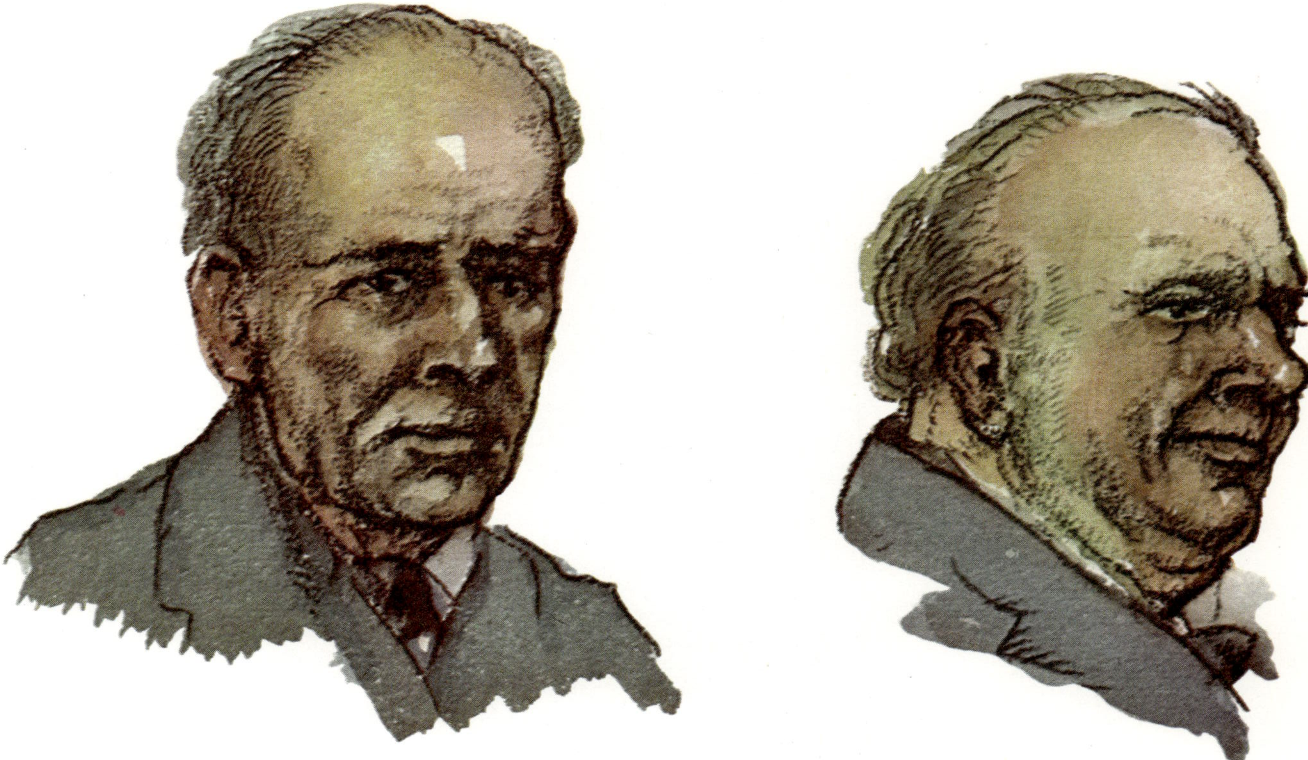

Tinted chalk drawings on watercolour paper. The drawings of the heads are fully modelled and then fixed. Colours used transparently: Light Red, Yellow Ochre and Payne's Grey.

THE ANATOMICAL APPROACH

It would be unrealistic in compiling a book which is devoted to faces and figures to exclude any mention of Anatomy. Faces are fashioned on the bony foundation of the skull, while figures are similarly constructed on the scaffolding of the skeleton, which in turn is covered and modified by the muscular system.

How much inside information is desired or deemed necessary to invest our pictorial heads and people with life, is a question that can only be answered by the individual reader. To some—perhaps the majority—a little knowledge, a passing glance, is all that they feel is required for their drawings to pass the required standard and achieve the "know how"! Others may be desirous of a closer look and when such curiosity is aroused as to just *how* and *why* our bodies work the way they do, a book which specializes on the subject is warmly recommended.

Such anatomical information however is beyond the scope of this little book which can only offer a helpful "digest" on the subject. I hope it will be sufficient to explain for instance that our features and the general configuration of the head is greatly influenced by the bony formation of the skull. My simplified diagrams of the part it plays will suffice to prove this point. Indeed it should be self evident when it is seen how superficial the bones of the cranium and lower jaw are in relation to the surface modelling of the features (see page 11).

When we come to examine the human figure, simple anatomical diagrams are less easy to synthesize or reconcile to the living person.

I have resorted again (as I did in *What Shall We Draw?*) to a tubular man in various positions, with such additional information as I now hope will narrow the gulf between the stiff and

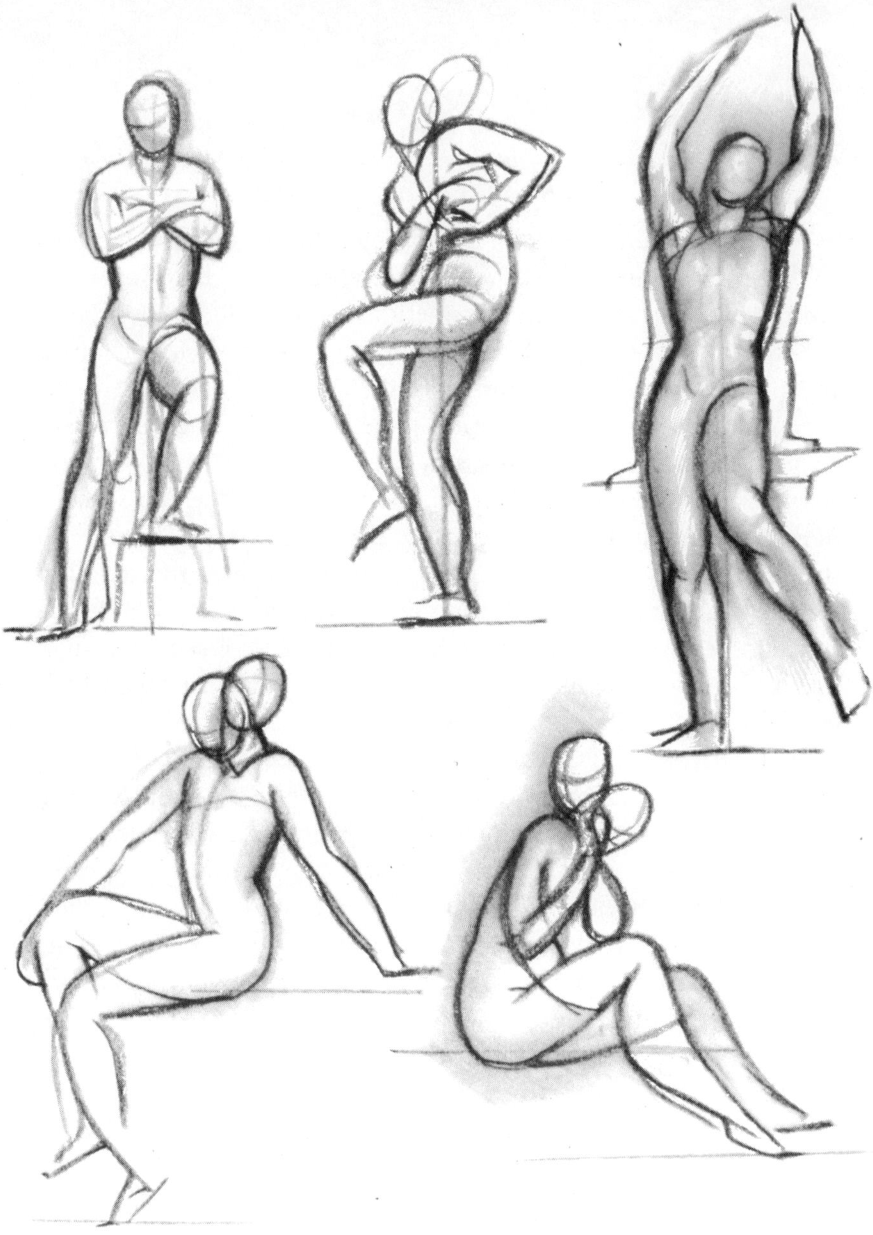

Some of the movements and positions of the human figure which cannot be followed by the robot formula.

mechanical *attitudes* of a robot and the subtle undulations and rhythmic movements of a human figure (see page 62).

These diagrams, if properly understood, will I believe be sufficient to enable the beginner to construct a figure which can in fact function in a human way and, when clothed, will be found to work!

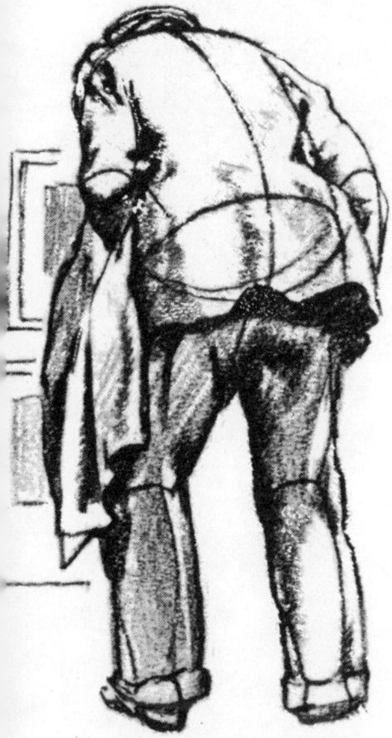

1. *Bending over to look down.*

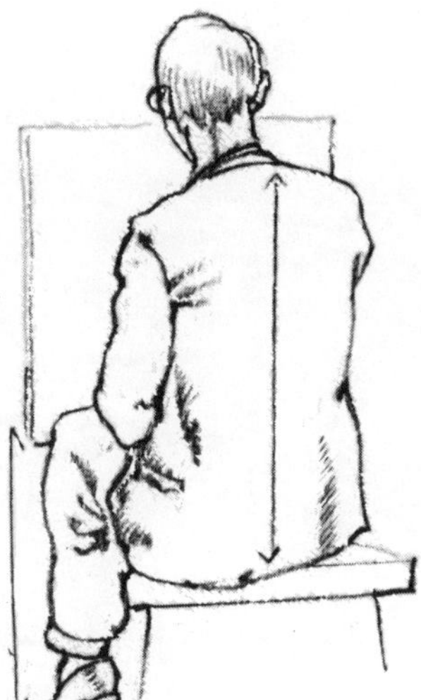

2. *Sitting to draw.*

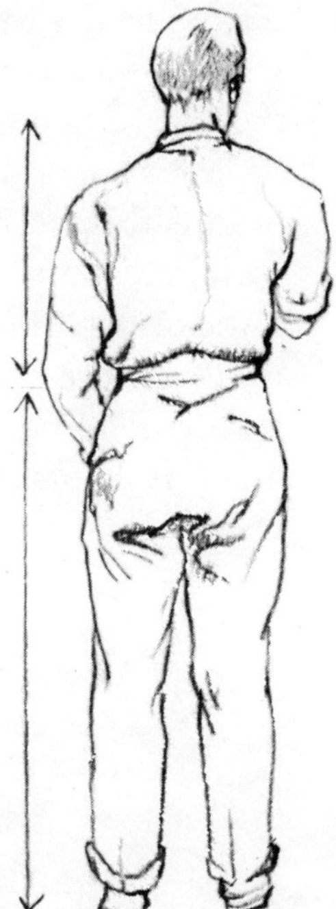

3. *Standing to glance sideways.*

FORESHORTENING

Although the student of faces and figures is happily relieved—may I say—of the apparent dread of perspective (which I have been at some pains to exorcize in this present series!) he has to meet the alternative challenge of *Foreshortening*, which at one time or another must be faced and overcome when the face or figure is portrayed in such a position that the features or limbs are no longer seen in profile; as when, for example, the head is thrown back, turned away, or looking down, and when a limb or the whole figure is in action. Indeed in most positions static or in motion, some part of the body will generally be found to need foreshortening, i.e. the arms or legs will project or recede. The best and most logical method for the beginner to adopt is to draw *just what you see*, and not what you know to be there.

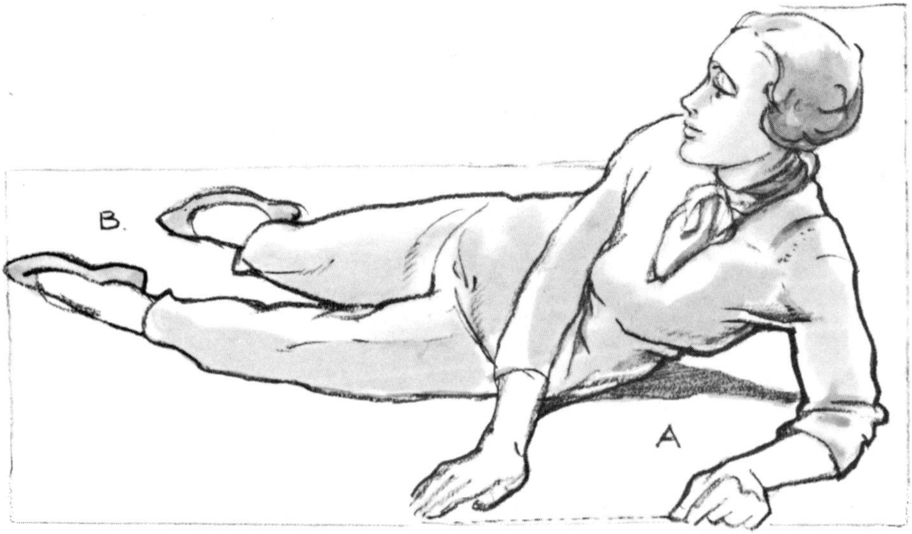

Shapes left between the legs and arms which help foreshortening (A, B).

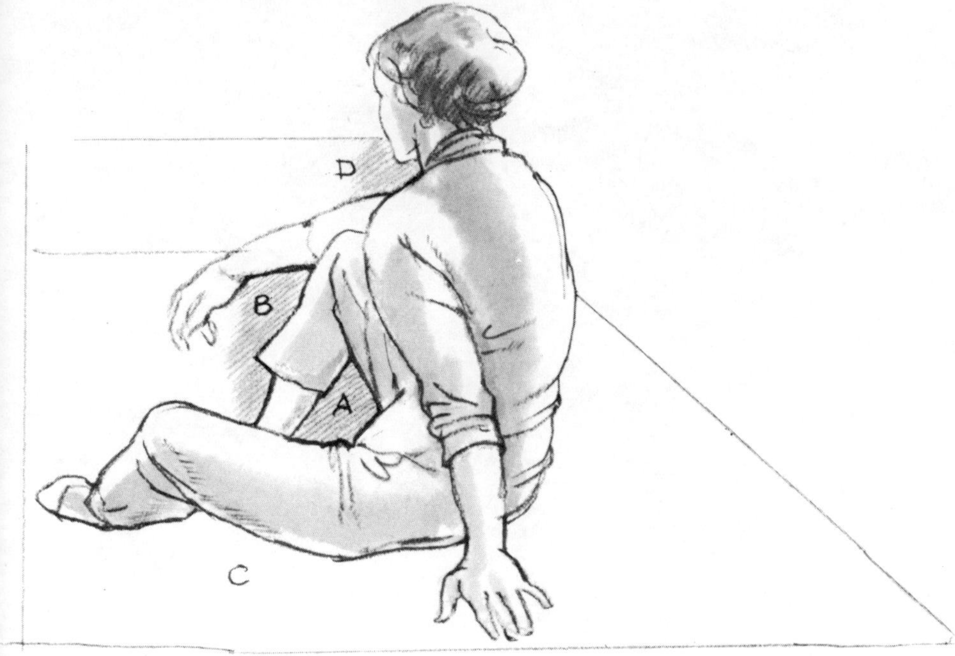

Shapes, A, B, C, D, especially A and B which determine the foreshortened position.

Draw the *shape* it makes and no more, even if you have to forget its normal length and thickness and function. And the beginner can achieve this by drawing the shapes *between* the foreshortened feature, i.e. the space between arms and body and that between the legs. A glance at the illustrations on pages 65-7 will show how this procedure works, for work it certainly does. In each case it will be seen that it is the surrounding or intervening spaces which determine the exact shape and size of the foreshortened form.

For while a knowledge of Anatomy can explain and aid the construction of the limb in *profile*, it can often hinder when projection or recession is required.

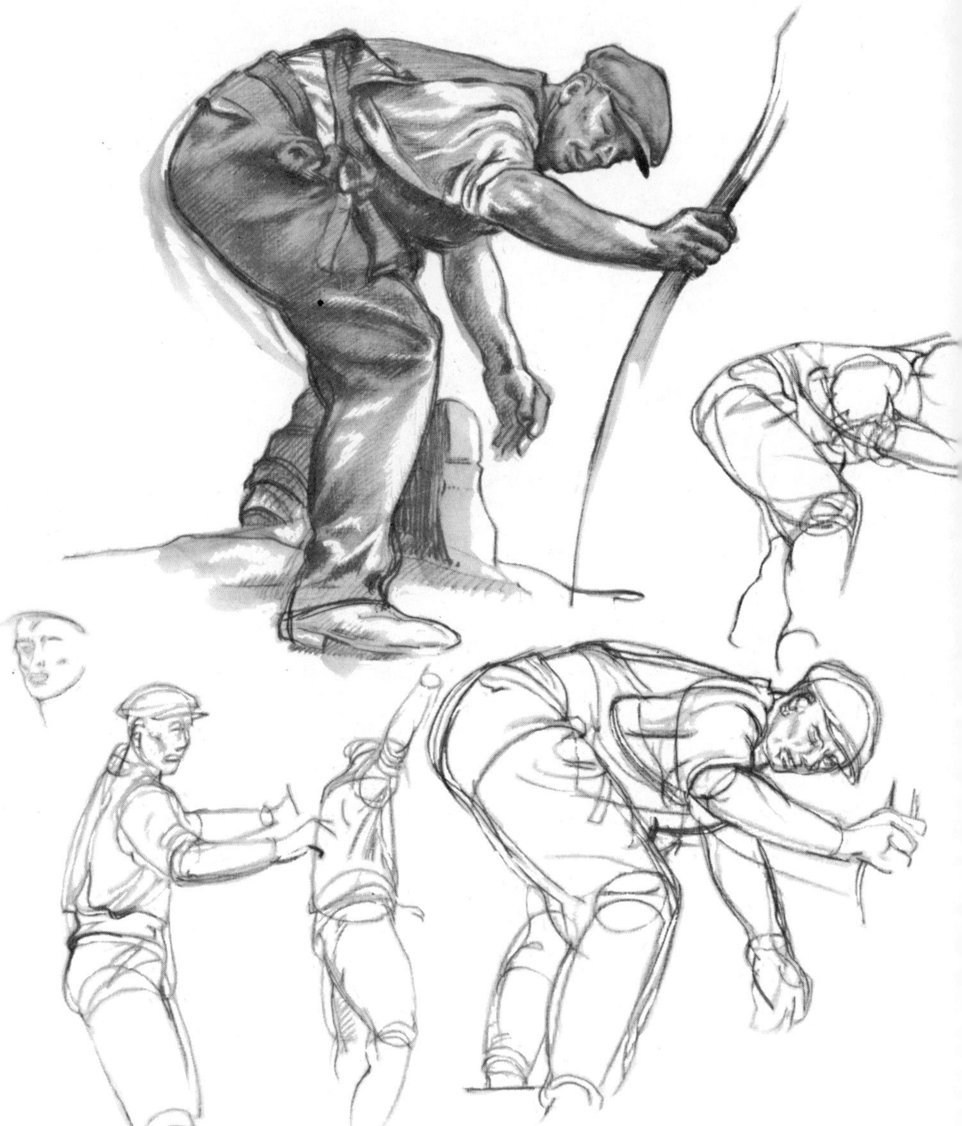

Foreshortening—shapes left.

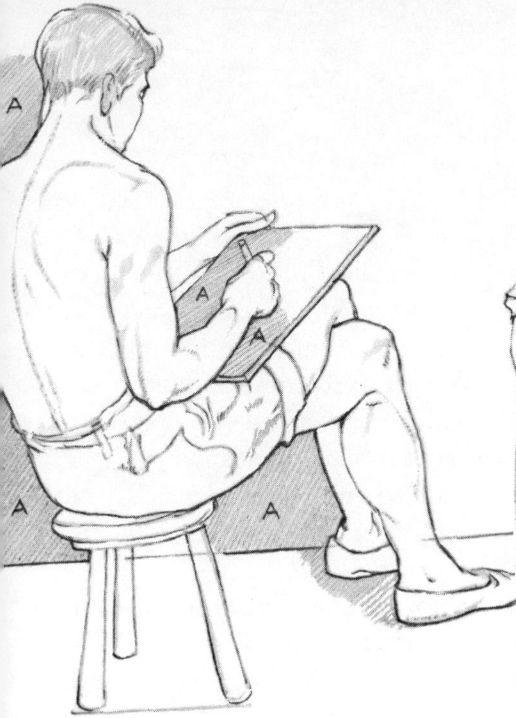

Foreshortening by drawing shapes between A.

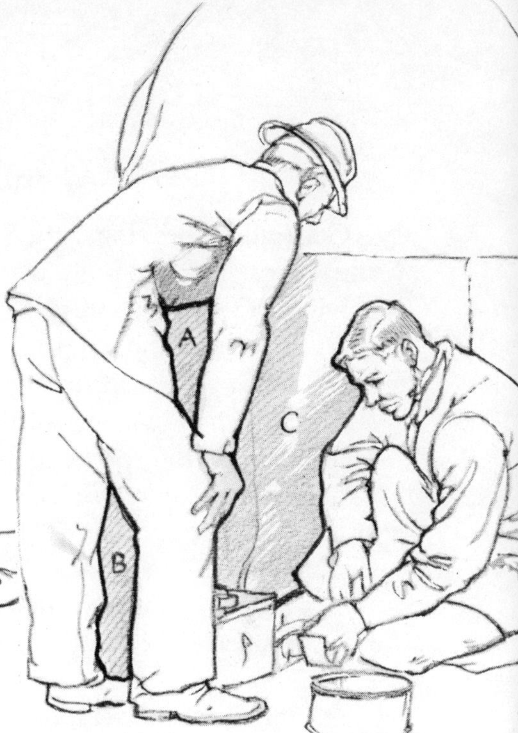

Shapes A, B, C, which will keep proportion and position between two figures.

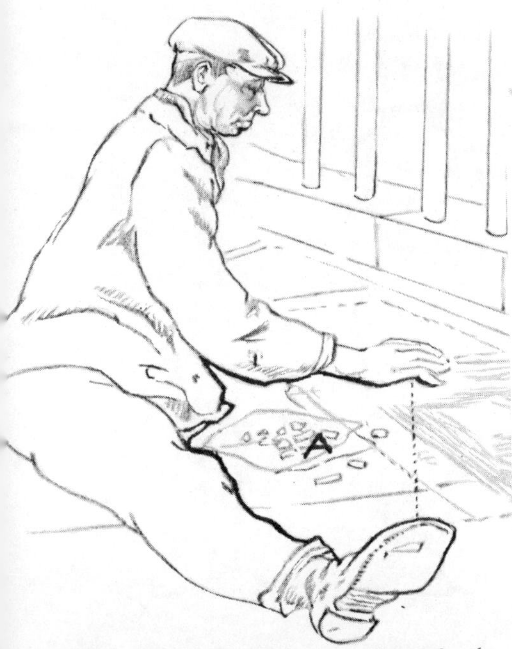

ne-legged pavement artist. Notice the shape left ween the under-arm, hand, lower leg and foot (A).

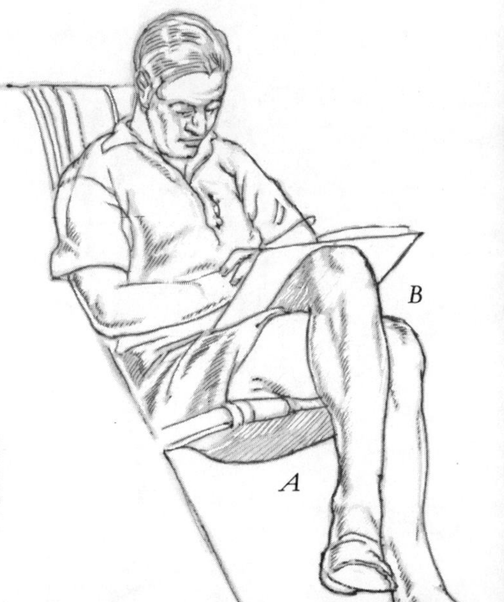

Shapes between A and B.

PROPORTION

Generally speaking, the male figure is broader, taller and more strongly built than the female (indeed the average height of the male appears to have increased noticeably over the years, if the size and length of the warriors suits of armour are a yardstick to go by). Naturally there are exceptions to every rule and we all know of many women who are taller and stronger than their male counterparts, but for purposes of studying their comparative characteristics, it is safe to envisage the male form as built on sturdier lines—squarer built in fact, is, I think, an apt distinction.

A well grown male displays this squareness in shoulders and hips, whereas the female form is constructed on eliptical lines—sloping shoulders, rounded hips, curves rather than angles, are characteristic of the outlines.

The entire bone construction of the female is more delicately assembled and articulates with more grace and rhythm.

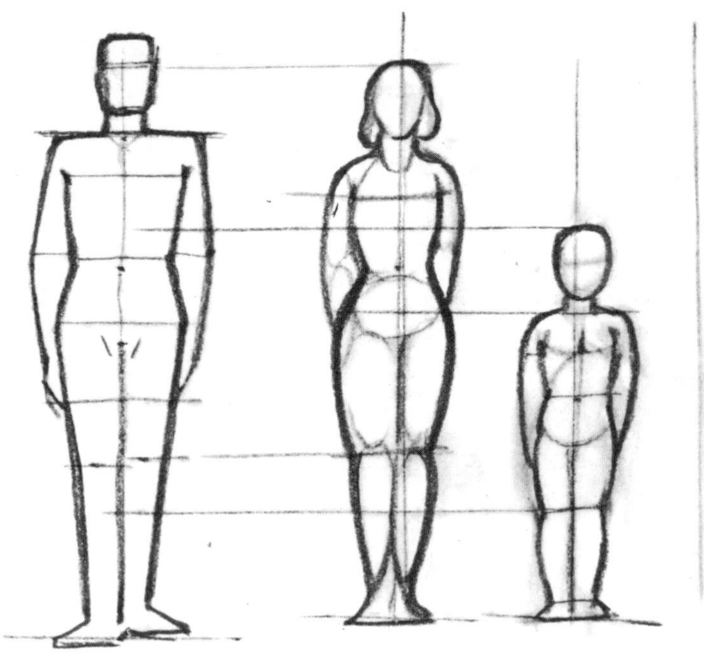

Male. *Female.* *Child.*

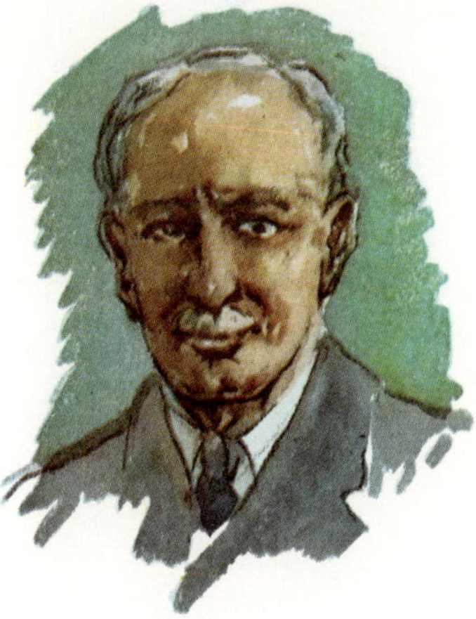

Accents strengthened by carbon.

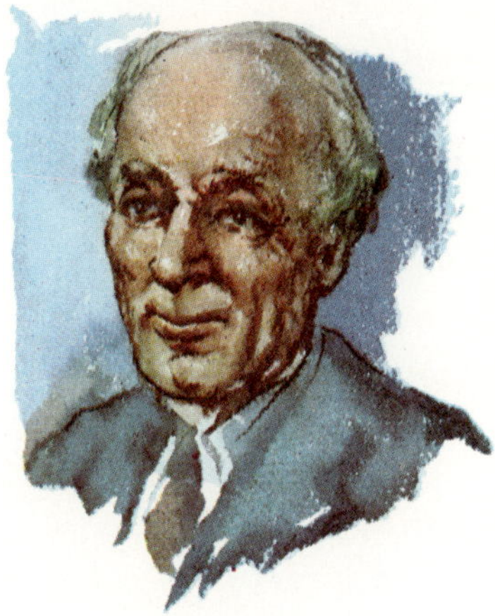

Pure watercolour painted on heavyweight paper, suitable for portraits of the elderly sitter.

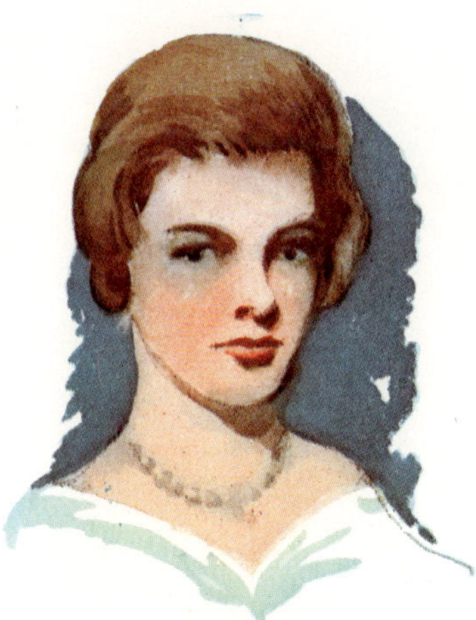

Pure watercolour over chalk drawing. The outline noticeably round the jaw is still to be erased.

Once this difference is understood, we can attack the drawing of the male in a more robust fashion than when depicting the form of the female, where our approach should be more sensitive and subtle. With regard to proportion of heads to bodies, children are very apt to draw the heads of grown-ups far too large in proportion to their figures. This may be accounted for by the fact that their own heads, up to a certain age, are larger and more mature than the rest of their bodies (incidentally it is because of this very fact that we grown-ups can always differentiate between youth and age, even when seen back view and at a distance). In this connection, it is interesting to notice the wilful blindness or ignorance of this fact in many of the Italian Primitive

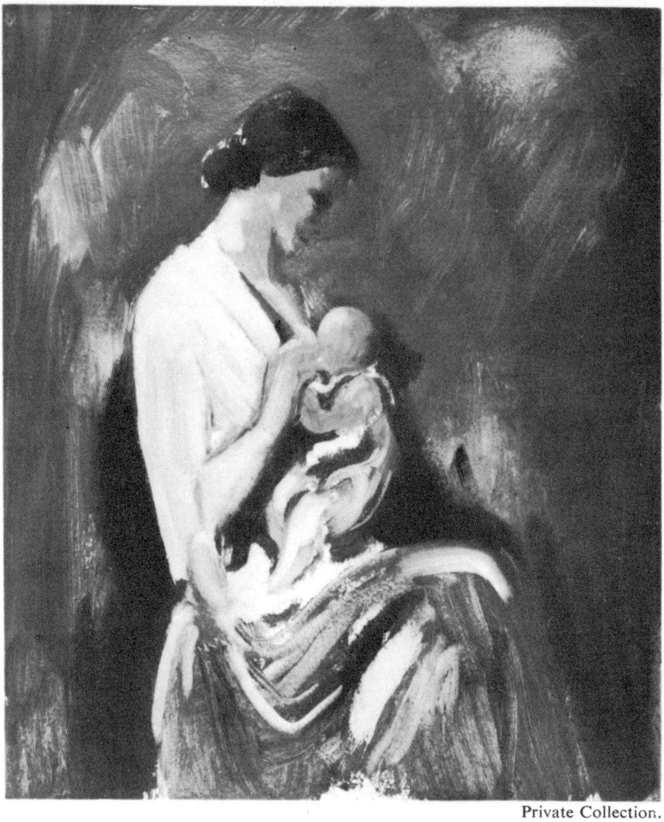

Private Collection.

Mother and child.

paintings depicting the Virgin and Child, where the infant Christ generally resembles a miniature man rather than a natural baby, just because the head is in proportion to the body as in an adult. It is not until the child reaches the "teens" that the body can be said to catch up with the head, and not until the twenties are reached does the adult balance of head to height occur. I remember being told as a student always to draw the head of an adult slightly smaller than it appeared and the feet much larger! There is sense in this, for in the first case dignity will be achieved and in the latter a good support will be offered for the preservation of this dignity! Moreover, I would add, not only the feet but the hands, for these too can so easily look like primitive little claws.

Place the base of the palm of your hand on your chin and extend your fingers to cover your face and you will find that three of your fingers will (or should) comfortably reach above your eyebrows! Few hands in a beginner's drawing could possibly reach higher than the tip of the nose (tiny female hands may be all very well for romance, but for pictorial emphasis they can look terribly ineffectual). Arms and legs of both sexes naturally vary considerably, but again we must generalize if artistic proportion is our yardstick. The normal length of the arm can be tested by holding it to the side of the body and when extended, the fingers will be found to reach about half way down the thigh. The upper and lower leg taken together are roughly the same length as the body, i.e. from the pit of the neck to the base of the trunk or torso.

Finally in proportion to the comparative height of the mature male and female figure ($8\frac{1}{2}$ heads go into a male—$6\frac{1}{2}$ heads to a height of a female), the shoulders of the male are slightly wider than that of the hips and in the female the opposite is *generally* observed. With these basic differences recognized, certain pitfalls in figure drawings, I hope, will be avoided.

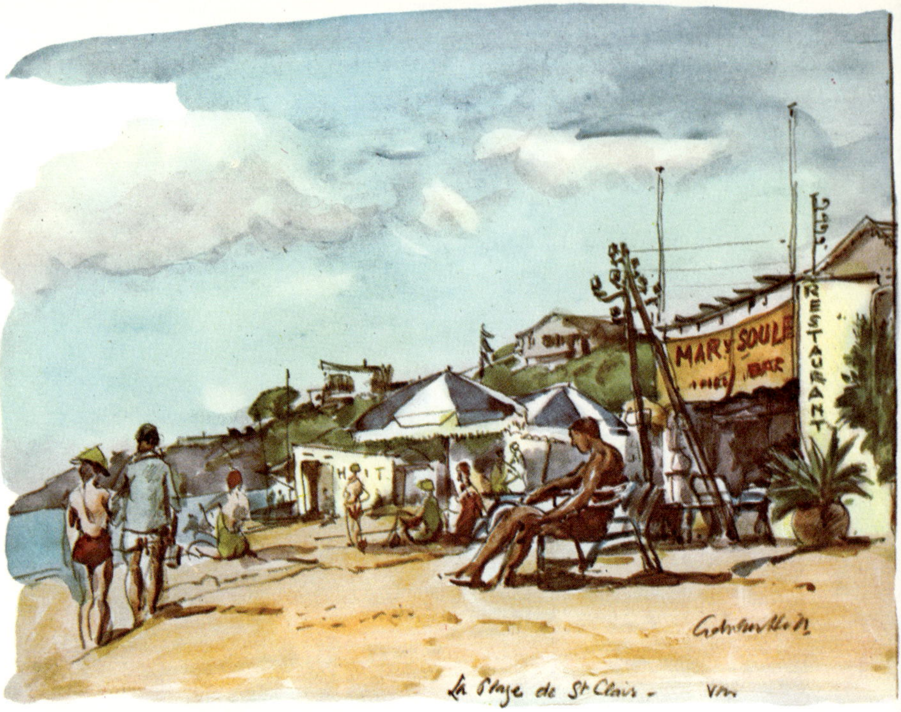
MARY SOULE
BAR
RESTAURANT
La Plage de St Clair

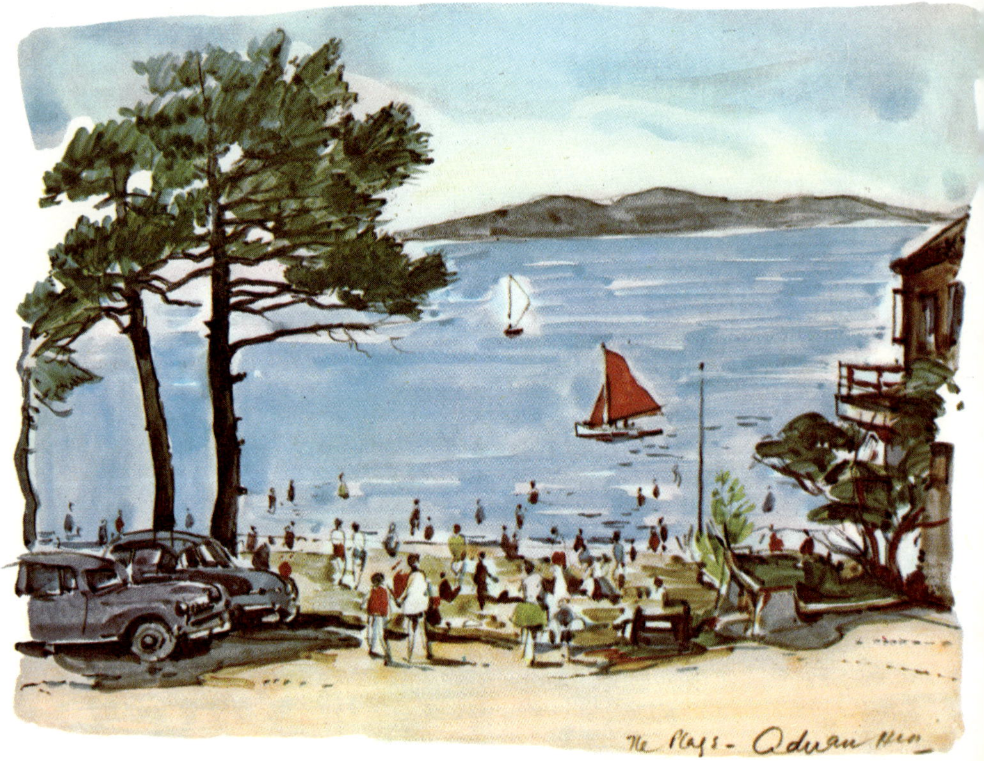

10 *Figures as Part of a Picture*

ALTHOUGH this portion of the book is devoted to figures, they must not be considered always as isolated subjects, single forms torn out of the context of the community, but rather as potential features which can be integrated into both landscape and interior pictures.

As a supporting interest, a figure—or figures—can invest the composition with a welcome vitality which only the human element can supply. This does not mean that either indoor subjects or scenes out of doors are necessarily incomplete without the introduction of people (Paul Nash never to my knowledge introduced a single human being into any of many landscapes), but that quite often the inclusion of a figure or two will enhance the surroundings and make the subject come alive.

Those readers who have braved the hazards of painting on the spot, know full well that it is not unusual to find that one is not alone! Not for long at any rate!

Within five minutes of arriving at the desolate and romantic pass of Glencoe in the Highlands a year or two back, another car had parked beside ours and, well, we were no longer alone.

And although I remember at first how much I resented this unwelcome intrusion, I was surprised to discover as the new arrivals left their car and started to explore the glen, that as a *pictorial accent*, these tiny figures—as they retreated into the middle distance—were of invaluable help when compared in size

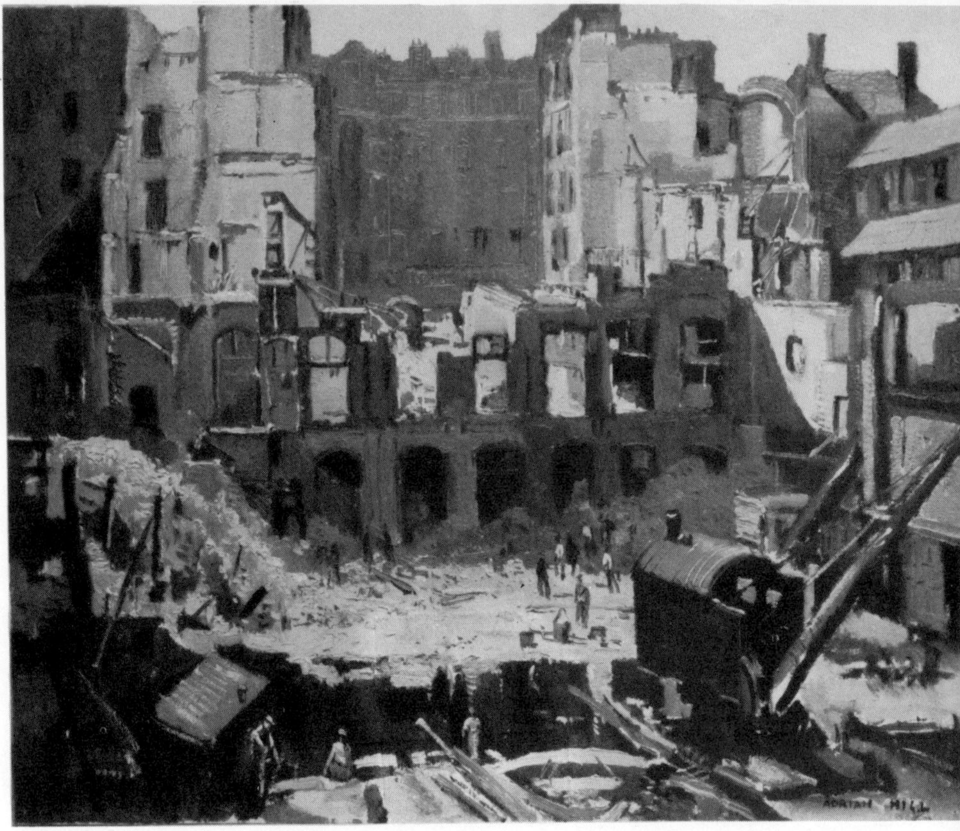

"Demolition"—Example of scene including figures.

with the towering heights of the surrounding mountains. Indeed it is for this very reason of their comparative heights with surrounding forms and trees, or buildings, that figures play such an important part, especially if emphasis of impressiveness is essential, i.e. the majesty of a forest tree or the height and dignity of a cathedral facade. In such cases the introduction of figures makes sure of this, as a glance at so many notable pictures by the Old Masters will confirm.

Here then is one reward for making many repeated studies of people. The experience we have gained in such study gives us confidence to take figures *in our stride* when we feel the need for

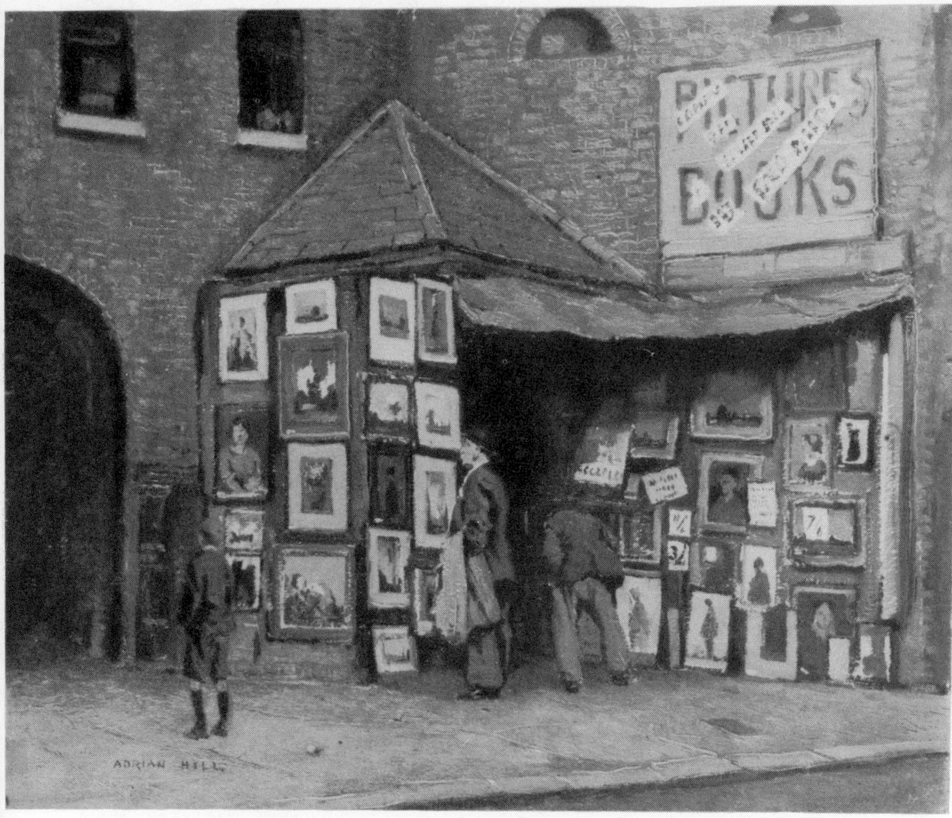

"Disappearing London"—painted from numerous pencil drawings and colour notes made on the spot.

bringing in the human element to complete our composition. Where to place them so that they appear naturally and how to paint them so that we *find them*, rather than their presence being forced upon us, is like every other problem of picture making, a matter of experience and experiment. I know some painters who, when in doubt about figures in a landscape, will put their paintings in a frame *behind glass*, and then try out their ideas on the glass itself—in this way they can see the effect without disturbing the actual painting, while making sure that the figure or figures will occupy the exact place in their composition; it is a tip worth passing on.

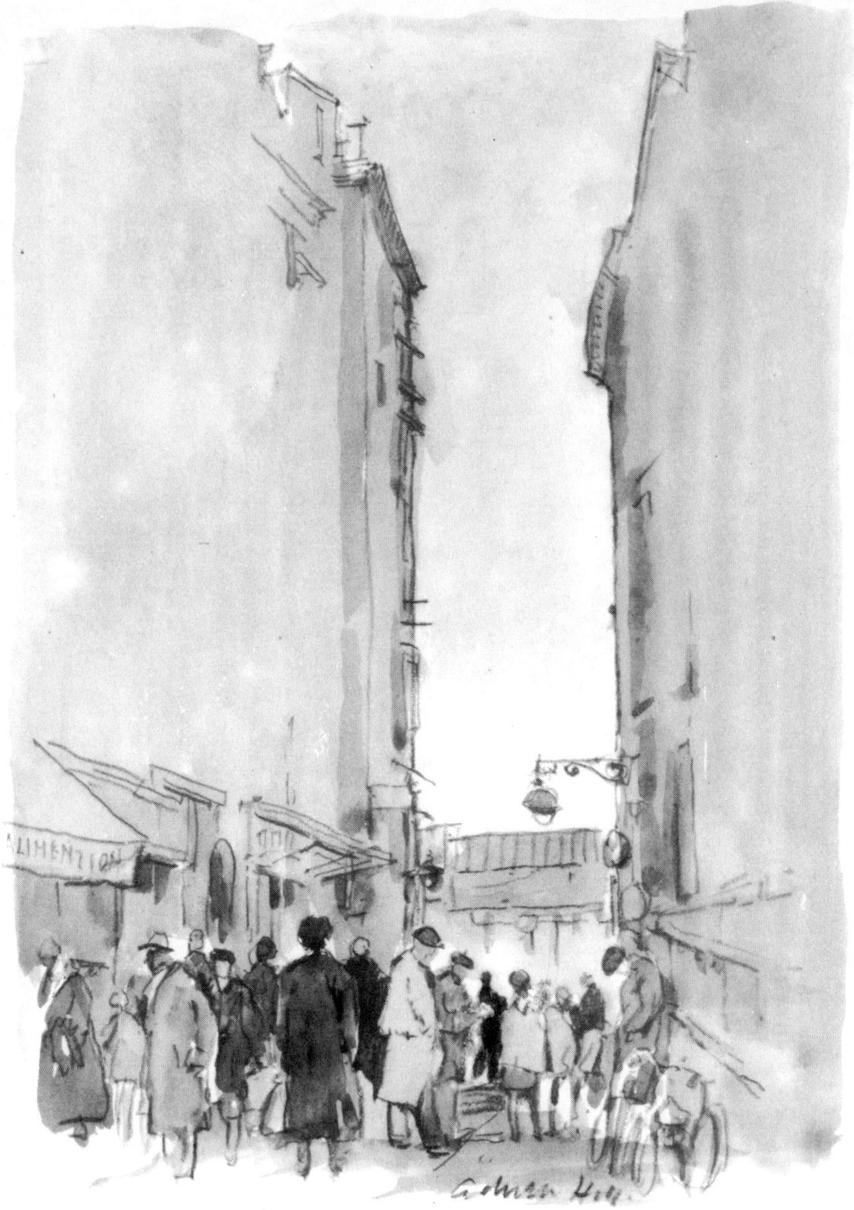

Street scene in Paris.

Conclusion

THE significant, and to some perhaps, sinister, metamorphosis discernable in the portrayal of the human head and figure, which is apparent in so many aspects of modern Art, may well pose the question as to the necessity of basing one's study of the human form on such traditional—even old fashioned—naturalistic data. In current exhibitions the human body is painted and sculptured with scant respect—or so it would seem—for what has been revered in the past as God's handiwork.

While it is easy to be biased and pontificate, I have, for my part a lurking sympathy for the young student who finds it difficult to reconcile the naturalistic principles of yesteryear with the abstract precepts of to-day, especially when the latter is becoming accepted and the former in danger of being rejected, or as we say, "on its way out".

In the end of course the choice must be a personal one. And to make the right decision you must surely know what it is you are abstracting from—what to simplify, what to retain and what to reject. When you can draw, paint or model a face and figure as they appear to the normal man and woman, you have a perfect right to turn and twist or torture them into any shape you sincerely consider to be more personal, more expressive of the modern age (or, dare I add perhaps more fashionable!).

But, and this must be underlined, you have no right to attempt this reconstruction or recreation until you have learnt and know

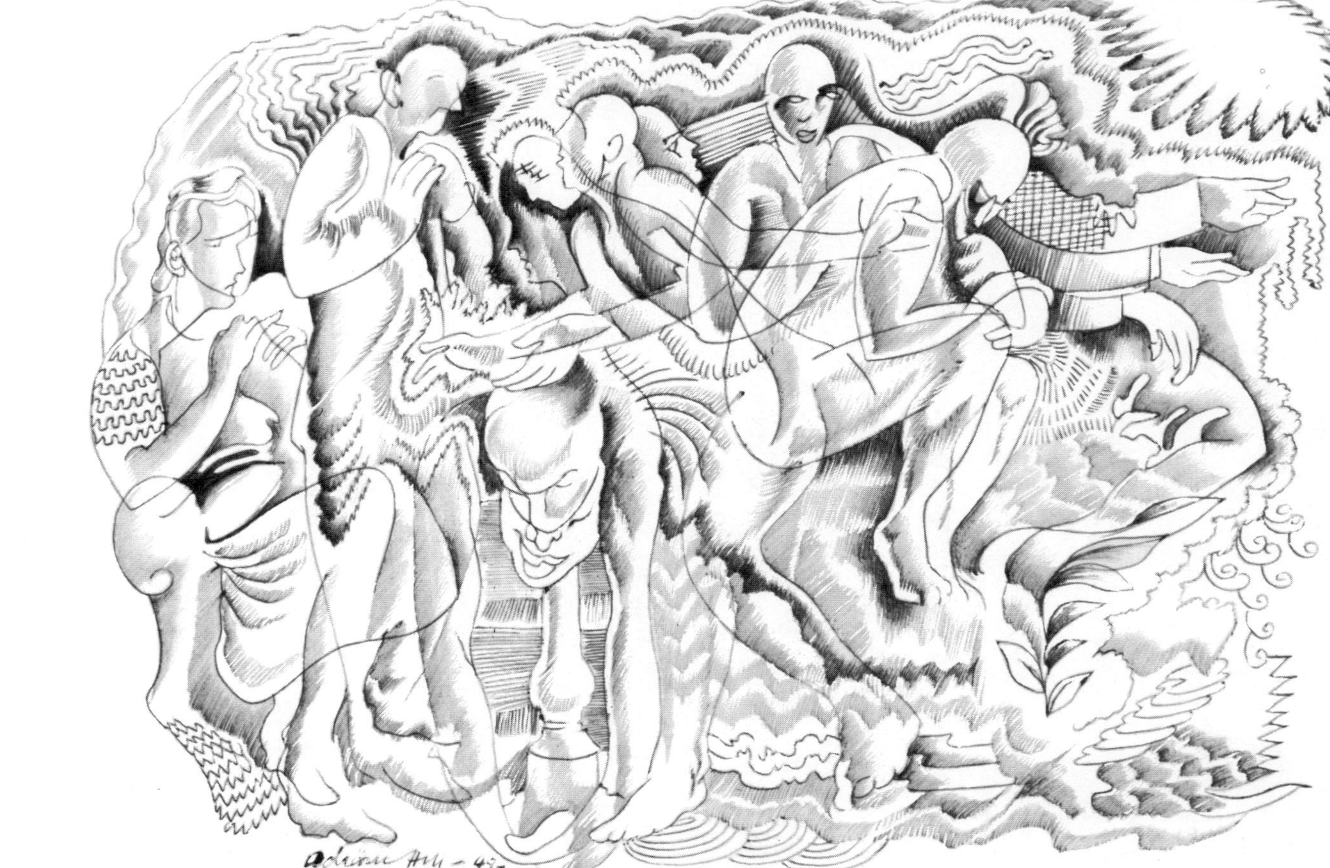

Abstract design in pen

all you can of the original structure from which to build afresh. And you will find that this disciplinary method of progress has been accepted by all the masters of the modern movements.

I hope this little book will help you on your way to the right choice, and when and how to make it. For I have shown perhaps sufficient evidence of my own efforts to solve this problem to absolve me from being a "diehard".

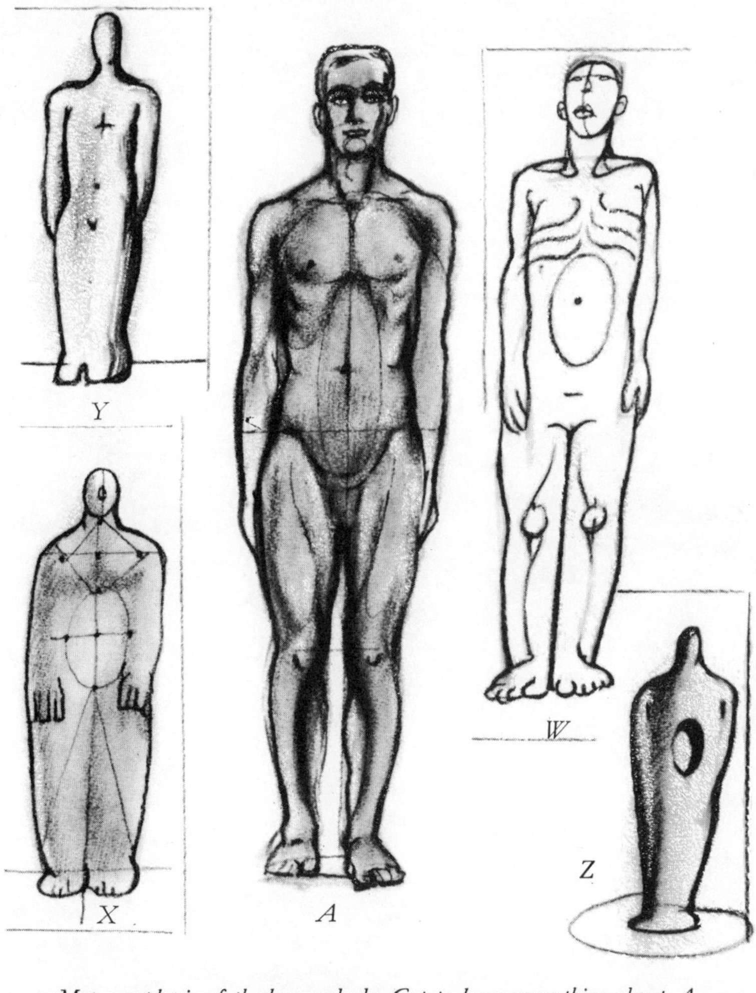

Metamorphosis of the human body. Get to know everything about A before experimenting with W, X, Y, and Z.